The Empowerment Paradox

THE

EMPOWERMENT

PARADOX

Seven Vital Virtues to
Turn Struggle Into Strength

BEN WOODWARD

LIONCREST
PUBLISHING

THE EMPOWERMENT PARADOX
Seven Vital Virtues to Turn Struggle Into Strength

ISBN 978-1-5445-0897-9 *Hardcover*
      978-1-5445-0896-2 *Paperback*
      978-1-5445-0895-5 *Ebook*
      978-1-5445-0898-6 *Audiobook*

Dedicated to my wife Kim and our seven children—
Ethan, Josh, Abbie, Sam, Toby, Noah, and Oliver.

CONTENTS

INTRODUCTION

I have a library filled with self-help books, many of which I acquired in the pursuit of greater strength, searching for increased understanding amidst my own personal struggles in life and the adversity it provided. There was a time when I desperately read through any guidance I could find, looking for anything that could bring meaning to the struggles I found myself dealing with.

Two recent books that found their way to my bookshelves seemed at first glance to contradict each other. One is *The Art of Happiness*, in which the Dalai Lama expresses the value of being happy and experiencing joy. The other is Jordan Peterson's *The Twelve Rules for Life*, which explains that life is not so much about happiness at all, but more about developing our character in the face of suffering.

These authors are not the first to address the inherent contradictions in joy and suffering from their given perspectives. People have long pondered the paradox of which carries more weight in human experience and personal growth—joy or suffering. Should we pay more attention to one than the other?

While the Dalai Lama explains that the purpose of life is to seek happiness and Dr. Peterson teaches that our purpose is centered on how we develop in the face of adversity—they do not, in fact, contradict each other. Meaning can be found through the experience of both joy and suffering, which are not found in isolation from each other. Each are accurate views of the world because joy and suffering are two sides of the same coin.

Striving for joy is a worthwhile endeavor, but it does not come without struggle and adversity. The Dalai Lama knows this well, as he continues to live in exile from his Tibetan homeland. It seems apparent that meaning and purpose in life are, in fact, inseparable from joy and suffering. Each can be analyzed separately, but in order for life to be fully realized, they must be lived as one.

THE SECOND-BEST THING

This interconnectivity of joy and suffering is one of many paradoxes of a fulfilling life, and one I have found exemplified by a friend of mine.

Andy Butterworth and I worked together for some years, during which his perspective on life intrigued me. He often walked with a cane and sometimes used a wheelchair due to injuries he'd sustained. Those conditions were only one facet of a very full life, which included extensive military training, two tours of the Falklands, an eventual career in IT, and a very happy and fulfilled marriage.

His injury, ironically, came after his time in the military in an accidental fall that broke his back. The doctors repaired the extensive damage by fusing pieces of his spine, which made matters worse rather than better. He married in a full body cast and set off on his new life needing care and a significantly different approach to the daily tasks of living.

I asked him once how often he experienced pain.

"Every day," he told me.

"Are you in pain now?"

"Yes," he said, remaining just as calm and composed as ever.

When I inquired further, he told me that it felt like his feet and legs were on fire, and that this was his normal state of being. Sometimes it felt manageable, and other times it overwhelmed him. On those days, he often worked remotely from the relative comfort of his home.

Remarkably, he also told me this: "I have come to appreciate that breaking my back was the second-best thing that ever happened to me—second only to meeting and marrying my wife. What it has demanded of me has shaped me into a person I never would have become otherwise."

The crucible of affliction had polished out the rough edges of the young kid he had been upon entering the military so many years before. When I watched my dear friend, who I worked with every day, it was difficult to comprehend just how much he had to overcome on a daily basis. At the same time, knowing what I did about affliction and perseverance, I could relate to just how much personal growth can emerge from even the darkest spaces.

I don't call attention to my friend's story to establish any kind of hierarchy of suffering. His story is remarkable not because of his degree of struggle, but because of his response to it.

It's important to realize that overwhelming struggle will not always lead to overwhelming victory. There is no guarantee attached to suffering. One person might discover similar strength of character through much less severe circumstances, while another might live with higher levels of chronic pain and feel completely buried and defeated by it. Still, another could feel buried under objectively lower levels of stress.

It's also an unfortunate reality that most people aren't willing to change until the pain of the problem becomes greater than the pain of their solution. I don't believe we need to hit what addicts call "rock bottom" before we can turn around. Nor is there a point of no return in which suffering becomes so great that joy is pushed out of reach.

Sometimes we grow due to adverse circumstances of our own making. Other times we grow due to circumstances outside of our control. And some of us are able to grow by learning from the experiences of others.

In many instances, my wife falls in the latter category, and I envy that about her. I tend to self-inflict most of my lessons. Yet the fact remains that each of us will face some level of adversity in our lives. How we experience adversity will be unique to our personality traits, our state of learning and understanding, and our circumstances at the time. The way we grow or suffer through the challenges of life depends entirely on our perspective. In that way, each of us can aspire to the level of my friend's excellent perspective and personal growth regardless of the life we're presented with.

TURNING STRUGGLE INTO STRENGTH

The paradox of empowerment is that it does not depend on our circumstances, though our circumstances directly affect the sense of strength and empowerment we attain. Life is marked by both joy and suffering, surrender and desire, knowledge and faith, and a grateful acceptance of the past encased within a patient and persistent eye on the future.

A wise CEO once said to me, "One thing I've learned about business is that you're always going into or coming out of a crisis. If you're smiling, I know what's around the corner for you."

Yet if we're asked to envision a happier future, it is often one that is stress-free. We imagine an emotional homeostasis where we have acquired enough wealth to remove strain that requires personal growth, where our relationships are fulfilling and engaging, and our physical health is in top condition. We see ourselves with a perfect and enviable work-life balance, the personification of everything good.

This vision of happiness, however, removes stress and strain, when in fact, it's those uncomfortable facets of reality that make happiness, fulfillment, and joy possible.

Alternatively, if we lose sight of the pursuit of happiness, we might engage only with the struggle and lose all sense of hope and joy.

In actuality, we need both as co-existing components of the same reality. An Olympian's joy can only be completely understood by others who have put in an Olympic amount of time and effort, and who have overcome the injuries and setbacks that brought the winner to that podium. Their triumphant joy is in direct proportion to their magnificent sacrifices. The exuberance felt when crossing the finish line goes hand in hand with the anguish of painful training. Similarly, being deeply and overwhelmingly in love feels that much more intense to a person who has felt the devastating, bitter pain of breakup and loss before.

Perspective is everything.

For the young people celebrating the turn of the new millennium on December 31, 1999, their joy was promoted by the media as the biggest global celebration anyone could imagine. But as my wife's grandmother so wisely acknowledged, older generations had a very different point of view. Paraphrasing, she said:

> "The biggest party that I've ever seen was when they announced the end of World War II. Everyone instinctively walked outside into the street when they heard the news. The emotion was palpable and overwhelming. It was something I will never forget. That was something to celebrate!"

She had lost her sister in the war. She and her husband had been separated during the fighting. She herself had been blown out of the window of an ammunition factory. By experiencing the ferocity of war, she more deeply felt the joy of its end.

The pursuit of happiness is a noble one, as long as we accept that it is found in the acceptance of struggle and the growth it can create. Similarly, the virtues that we seek to obtain are complex because our struggle is complex. They take time because growth takes time. Like a tree that grows to bear fruit, there is a maturing process that happens over the course of many seasons.

Though not all of us will sustain terrible injuries and live with incessant pain throughout our lives like my friend or experience the atrocities of war like my wife's grandmother, we can all grow through whatever suffering we're presented with and find joy in the midst of it.

THE SEVEN VIRTUES

It's natural to hope to eliminate struggle, whether it is illness, interpersonal strain, or the pressure of deadlines, client demands, or perpetual, entrepreneurial risk. Yet when we accept the reality of crisis, we can more fully appreciate the joy found on the other side. Thirteenth-century poet Rumi put it beautifully as this:

> "Sorrow prepares you for joy. It violently sweeps everything out of your house, so that new joy can find space to enter. It shakes the yellow leaves from the bough of your heart, so that fresh, green leaves can grow in their place. It pulls up the rotten roots, so that new roots hidden beneath have room to grow. Whatever sorrow shakes from your heart, far better things will take their place."

I believe there are seven vital virtues that, if developed over time, help us to shake out the old and make way for new growth. These virtues are:

1. A disciplined heart
2. An educated mind
3. Nourished faith
4. Well-practiced patience
5. A liberated past
6. Diligent work
7. Willful surrender

We'll explore each virtue in detail in the second half of the book. As you can see, they are not simple tasks, nor are they linear. Each one leads to the next and back to the ones that came before. In fact, it is often the cyclical repetition and endurance of the struggle that entrenches and ingrains the lesson.

These virtues require self-reflection. They demand that we stretch outside of our comfort zones. But here is the joy: the benefits of each will transfer across every aspect of your life. They make you a better person and a more insightful, caring spouse or partner. They make you a better parent. A stronger entrepreneur. A wiser and more empathic leader. A more diligent employee. A confident, strong, visionary person who is equipped to become who they truly want to be. Yes! Wherever your life places you today—these virtues will prepare you to cultivate joy from sorrow and step into the fullest version of yourself.

HAVE YOU BEEN BURIED OR PLANTED?

The question, then, is how some people are able to develop these virtues with an eye on the future rather than becoming bogged down under present struggle. How can we become empowered enough to go through terrible circumstances while remaining convinced that they are among the best things that have ever happened to us? The power is found in changing our perspective. It is the difference between being buried in isolation or, like a seed, planted with intention and great potential.

I've found in the past that my colleagues and I would frequently use the word "buried" to describe stressful circumstances, especially in a work context. We're swamped, snowed under, and feeling like work has piled on top of us. If we took the time to elaborate, it might be that we feel overwhelmed or out of control. There's an element of hopelessness or despondency expressed in those feelings.

Yet if we look to nature as an example, only a seed that is planted and covered in dirt can draw nutrients from the soil and grow to its full potential. A seed that is dropped to the ground from a tree only stands a chance of growth. It needs to be buried by the elements in order to take root.

The same is true for us. The adversities that seem to bury us under may be the very conditions we need to grow and take root. Perhaps a deeper sense of struggle comes with an element of design meant to help us develop stronger roots as we emerge into better versions of ourselves.

This is the context from which I will frame the empowerment paradox in this book, for if there is to be meaning in life, there must be meaning within the suffering. Time may heal all wounds, but it seems evident that time also wounds all proverbial heels. There is no escaping suffering, yet there is also joy to be found when we are patient, humble, and accepting of our circumstances.

I would rather see us identify with the seed when we feel buried and left in the dark than to feel isolated in our suffering. I would rather us look for the nutrients of virtue and lessons learned than to remain dormant and unchanged. I would rather us feel planted, hopeful, and open to the great potential of our lives.

A LIFE EMPOWERED BY ADVERSITY

The life that I have now is not the one I expected to have. For example, I did not plan to reunite with my father after years and years apart, only to discover crimes he had committed that I had to bring to light in order for justice to be done. No one wants to send their dad to prison, but that is what life demanded of me.

In my career—from design work to management, to presiding over global companies, to consulting companies experiencing crisis or wonderful transformation—I found great success as well as great struggle, all of it requiring me to learn and adapt in order to meet the requirements of the circumstances I faced. I share some of these stories in the chapters to come, ranging from my victories and defeats in childhood to challenges and achievements in life and business.

I share them with you in order to explore the choices we have and to help answer a difficult and pressing question: what should we do with this life that we've been given?

Do we want to allow the pressure of suffering and struggle to choke out our proverbial nutrients so that we wither and die, or do we want to grow where we are planted? This is a question no one can answer for us. There are some parts of life that we cannot delegate out, no matter how good our managerial skills. Once we grasp that our lives are our own unique opportunities to grow, we become empowered to grow into the best versions of ourselves.

My premise is not that we have to ensure hardship, nor that we should seek to attract a life free of it, but that we can become better versions of ourselves due to the coexistence of both joy and pain. Perhaps, by the end, this book will join others on shelves like mine, with dog-eared pages and margin notes that point to a life empowered by adversity rather than crippled by it.

Part I

THE PARADOXES OF A MEANINGFUL LIFE

The tree that never had to fight
For sun and sky and air and light,
But stood out in the open plain
And always got its share of rain,
Never became a forest king
But lived and died a scrubby thing.

The man who never had to toil
To gain and farm his patch of soil,
Who never had to win his share
Of sun and sky and light and air,
Never became a manly man
But lived and died as he began.

Good timber does not grow with ease:
The stronger wind, the stronger trees;
The further sky, the greater length;
The more the storm, the more the strength.
By sun and cold, by rain and snow,
In trees and men good timbers grow.

Where thickest lies the forest growth,
We find the patriarchs of both.
And they hold counsel with the stars
Whose broken branches show the scars
Of many winds and much of strife.
This is the common law of life.

—DOUGLAS MALLOCH, "GOOD TIMBER"

Chapter 1

BURIED AND DORMANT

PARADOX: ACCEPTANCE OF OUR CIRCUMSTANCES GIVES US STRENGTH TO CHALLENGE THEM

After our sixth child was born, my wife experienced postnatal depression for the first time ever. She went right to the doctor to get the help she needed, but of course, these things don't just go away. There were still some long nights to get through, filled with anxious thoughts and depressive insomnia. To her surprise, I had a wealth of resources for her. I pulled out books from my shelf and pointed to well-worn chapters. I empathized with what she was feeling and shared how I tried to cope when similar thoughts had plagued me. I even recorded some messages for her to listen to at night when the darkness felt heaviest, and she didn't want to wake me.

I could relate to her depression shockingly well.

"Ben," she asked me one day, "How do you know so much about this?"

I shrugged and told her, "I've felt this way, off and on, for about seven years."

Upon discovering just how badly I had suffered in private, she dragged me to the doctor.

Swings of depression had gone on so long that they became my normal. In my mind, there was nothing to see a doctor for, because I believed I was learning to cope on my own. It was a personal discomfort, but I saw no reason to bother anyone else with it—my wife hadn't even known what was going on.

When my moods swung to the opposite side of the pendulum, I felt great and didn't want that to go away. When they were stable, I didn't see a need for help. I could cover up the depression long enough to get back to those higher points, hiding and masking my condition at each variation enough that I thought I could manage in self-imposed isolation.

It wasn't until an English football coach was lost to suicide that I saw the potential end I was headed toward.

As the news story unfolded, the broadcasters relayed the coach's private, catastrophic depression. It was heartbreaking to watch. People desperately wanted a second story to break. They wanted to see a hidden life no one knew about, a devastating blackmail situation that he couldn't escape. After all, he had a great career and always appeared to be happy and doing well. He had been at a charity event the night before, engaged, social, and smiling. But there was no second story driving his untimely death, only an ongoing struggle with mental health.

His struggle was my own.

I thought back to the events I'd attended recently. If that news-reel had been focused on me, they could find similar accounts of a pleasant social presence. I was often on stage, playing the role of motivator and educator, making the audience laugh and cry and feel inspired. I had a prosperous career, happy marriage, and wonderful, healthy children we were raising in a lovely home. I traveled the world, looked healthy and fit, and by all accounts, seemed to enjoy a beautiful life. Yet on the inside, I was dying.

For the first time, I saw the gravity of my situation. There was nothing to separate me from that coach, and I needed to get the help that could literally save my life.

Unfortunately, many mental health diagnoses take time and a fair amount of trial and error. Not only is there the diagnosis period, which often requires a process of elimination, but another process for finding the right medication, and still more for the proper dosage. It takes time for each new dose to stabilize, for side effects to emerge, and then to evaluate and do it all over again if things need to adjust. Five years and one misdiagnosis of chronic depression later, a diagnosis of bipolar disorder type II gave me an accurate picture of what was going on inside my body and brain. More importantly, I had a path toward treatment and recovery.

Understanding the nature of bipolar disorder helped me to better appreciate the natural ebb and flow of life. I began to separate the feeling of a bad day that got me down from the disproportionate, overwhelming, crippling darkness that sometimes came in waves. That kind of depression, which my wife and I came to refer to as "bipolar low," destroys any sense of hope and vitality. It leaves you believing there is no longer a purpose to life.

My wife learned to ask, "Are you low right now, or are you bipolar low?" And, "Are you good, or are you bipolar good?" Meanwhile, my mother-in-law shared a very different concern: "How do we know what's the real you and what's the bipolar you?"

The truth is that it's all me. This is the lot I've been given, and I've finally come to accept it in a realistic way. The years that I spent alone in my suffering were not acceptance at all, but resignation. Kim modeled a realistic acceptance of her circumstances and the challenge required to overcome them, while I believed for far too long that I had to either ignore or absorb the effects of my illness.

In truly accepting the life that I have, compared with trying to force a reality that I had hoped to have, bipolar has become something of a superpower. My capacity to empathize and understand the struggles of others has been significantly augmented through rich personal experience. I am more patient when others struggle, understanding the road of suffering and recovery like Bill Murray's *Groundhog Day*. I feel their aches and hopes, disappointments and relief, and I manage my own feelings now better than ever before. These are lessons uniquely taught to me by my disorder. I wouldn't trade them for anything, even knowing the darkness it took to bring them to me.

As long as I clung to the life I wanted and expected, I felt buried, powerless, and crushed under my condition, always trying to make it go away and never gaining any ground. With time, distance, and growth, I now see that I had simply been planted in the ground, laying dormant for the time when I could draw from my experience and nurture great personal growth.

This is the first and very critical step in our journey to greater empowerment. Before we can cultivate the virtues of greater strength in ourselves, we have to first face our darkness, embrace and appreciate the value it brings to us, and accept our present reality—not our interpretation of a preferred one.

> "I'd give all the wealth that years have piled, the slow result of life's decay, to be once more a little child for one bright summer day."—Lewis Carroll, *Solitude*

MEANING FOUND IN ADVERSITY

The depths of despair found in untreated mental illness can also be felt in grief, post-traumatic stress disorders, a terminal diagnosis, or any number of physical and emotional traumas. These events stand as very real obstacles to hope, magnificent in size and terrifying in scope.

I could venture into the details of a particularly suicidal moment or the hypomania that took me off the rails on the other end of the spectrum, but I have my experience, and you have your own. There is no threshold for events that "qualify" as a struggle, and there is no struggle so big that it cannot be integrated into an empowered life. For this reason, the question is not one of circumstance, but of the actions we take in response to circumstance.

My bipolar diagnosis, while not something I would have expected or chosen, was one of the most thrilling bits of news I could have gotten. I went from lost and frustrated with no purpose behind my suffering to having a context to place it in. The language I was given for how I felt gave me meaning and a direction for my response. For example, I could learn my triggers and begin to look for early indicators of an episode in one direction or the other. The more I understood my condition, the more I could manage it. As I regained control of my emotions, I gained control of my life as well.

That wonderful relief was juxtaposed against the realization that the suffering wasn't going to end. No matter how sincerely I wanted it to go away, my desires couldn't create new circumstances. Acceptance and surrender were my only path to recovery and management.

One psychiatrist wisely told me, "You can't educate yourself out of this, Ben. This is your lifelong reality. So what are you going to do about it?"

We can choose to allow ourselves to be blown about with every wind of adversity, becoming directionless and out of control, a victim of fate and circumstance. We can also choose to continue ignoring our stressors until we implode one day in a spectacular tragedy. But only by facing our stressors directly, learning from them, and integrating those lessons into our lives, can we unlock the benefits they hold.

Acceptance can often turn our biggest struggles into our superpowers.

I believe, through time and a great deal of hard lessons learned, that we can take responsibility for our circumstances by choosing how we're going to grow from them. We can draw from what buries us, like a seed drawing nutrients from the soil, knowing growth is happening even when the fruits of an empowered life are not yet visible.

Please understand this: taking responsibility for our circumstances isn't about owning someone else's choices if we are struggling because of someone or something else outside of our control. A seed planted in dirt needs to accept that, in most cases, how it got there is irrelevant. Taking responsibility for our lives is choosing to accept what we do about it once we see where we are.

Similarly, at the heart of personal empowerment is the necessity of time. A tree does not grow overnight, nor is it in full bloom for the entirety of the year. If we skip our slow maturation process for the sake of a quick sprout of instant gratification, we miss the fruit that time and patience would have yielded.

Too much of pop culture today is invested in quick solutions. Modern gurus champion the pursuit of wealth, promising that a carefree life built on acquisition will bring happiness and meaning. We want quick meals, short exercise routines, and a fast-track to purpose and empowerment. But the virtues that empower a meaningful life come at a price—not the least of which is time. Our answers are not going to come in a moment any more than they will come without adversity.

Adversity shapes our lived experience, and experience nurtures patience and growth over time so that we're better equipped to face new adversity when it appears, in a virtuous circle of growth toward the person we have the potential to be.

So, I'm afraid my message is not themed in pop culture popularity. I am not offering fast, formulaic fixes for our problems or glorious victory from small sacrifices on our part. What I am offering is the real deal, time-tested in great adversity and joy alike, if you choose to accept it.

THE PURITANS, THE VICTORIANS, AND THE MILLENNIALS

As much as we tend to envision a future free of stress, we often look back at childhood with a similar idealism. We think of it as an innocent and lovely time, free from stress and worry. Lewis Carroll said it well: "I'd give all the wealth that years have piled, the slow result of life's decay, to be once more a little child for one bright summer's day." In general, we associate childhood with a more pleasant way of being.

Our first challenge along our path of progress is to acknowledge that this idealism is not reality. From a position of psychology and the sciences, the concept of childhood innocence is vague and undecided. There's no baseline of what it should be, developmentally. Rather, our perception of childhood is shaped by cultural influences that shift through the ages.

Consider the Puritans, for example, who viewed childhood from a staunchly religious perspective. As a result of the fall of Adam, they believed all mankind was lost and in need of redemption. Children, as a natural consequence, were in the precarious situation of an immediately fallen, vulnerable state, before being conscious enough to seek said redemption. They needed the strong influence of an adult who could guide—or rather, control—them until that time. This prohibited or heavily limited the childhood experiences that we now consider to be wonderful. Play and fun were sinful things that would only entrench the fallen state.

As we moved into the mid-nineteenth century, more positive associations with children were accepted. Childhood became a time of freedom, creativity, spontaneity, happiness, and yes, innocence. The adult's role was to shield that innocence from all outside influences, keeping the child from experience, tragedy, suffering, and trial as long as possible—at least for those children born to families wealthy enough to preserve this privilege. The privilege of the minority was taught as standard for all.

The literature of the Victorian age reflects these ideals, with Kingsley's *Water Babies*, George MacDonald's *At the Back of the North Wind*, and of course Lewis Carroll's *Alice's Adventures in Wonderland* in the 1860s, stretching all the way to J.M. Barrie's *Peter Pan* famously refusing to grow up. These stories have a hold on us to this day, perhaps as a vicarious escape from the realities of adulthood back into a sheltered childhood that is free of difficulty. If we could only remain in perpetual childhood—if we could attract a reality that removes the bulk of our responsibility and struggle—then life would be better. Do you relate?

Unfortunately, we can never "go home" to childhood again. Try as we might to envision a life free of stressors, we can never return to a simpler, more sheltered and supportive time. Necessary losses must occur if necessary gains are to be made. In other words, growing up includes giving something up—namely, innocence.

At the core of innocence is the absence of knowledge and experience. This is the foundation of the Puritanical approach to child-rearing. Adam and Eve were, in their story, innocent in the Garden of Eden. When they partook of the fruit of the tree of knowledge and good and evil, they were endowed with knowledge and no longer considered innocent. This was humanity's great fall and the source of condemnation that justified all kinds of violence and repression in their minds.

We may perhaps agree that the Puritans were misguided, but we must ask ourselves whether the Victorians got it right.

The first clue is that childhood for the working class was already very different from their wealthier counterparts. The next is that, as much as we pine for the opposite to be true, most children's lives are far from stress-free. The ideals of Victorianism were often based on escapism rather than depictions of reality. As Kimberley Reynolds wrote for the British Library, "There is a notable tendency in some of the best-known Victorian fantasies for child characters to die in this world in order to be reborn… or to stay children forever elsewhere…" with poor children written out of view or "built into literary ciphers."[1]

If we insist on holding on to Victorian ideals of childhood, then we must frustratingly hold the double standard based on class, as well.

In the United States alone, 43 percent of children are in low-income households, with 21 percent below the federal poverty threshold.[2] What must it be like for these children to hear that childhood should be all about innocence and freedom from stress and worry, heartache and struggle? What does it say when nearly half of our children experience the household stress of keeping food on the table and clothes on their backs, if not that classism is as alive now as it was in the Victorian era?

For children ages twelve to eighteen, 20 percent have reported being bullied. Thirty percent admit to having bullied others, and over 70 percent have acknowledged witnessing bullying

---

1   Kimberley Reynolds, "Perceptions of childhood," British Library, May 2014. https://www.bl.uk/romantics-and-victorians/articles/perceptions-of-childhood.

2   National Center for Children in Poverty, "Child Poverty," Accessed Online, January 2020. http://www.nccp.org/topics/childpoverty.html.

taking place.[3] Approximately 19 million children in America live with just one parent.[4] The impact of divorce or single-parent homes means less time with a parent, loss of economic security, increased chance of poverty, loss of emotional security, decreased social and psychological maturation, and so many more ills.[5] The average first exposure to pornography is at the age of eleven, and 94 percent of kids have been exposed to it by the age of fourteen.[6]

Each of these are waystations where the ideal of innocence is lost, and that's without getting into statistics around abuse, loss of loved ones, or chronic illness and disease.

In reality, there is no line of demarcation where nature protects us from any suffering, hurt, or ill will from other people, and our best intentions to preserve that imaginary line don't always create the best results. Before becoming a parent, I set a goal that I would never need to say sorry to any of my children. My wish was born of good intent. I wanted to get it right from the moment that they were born. But I've had to apologize to my kids countless times—and I've learned that this is a positive thing. Acknowledging my faults and flaws and demonstrating a willingness to learn and ask for forgiveness is good parenting, far more than the perfectionistic ideal I had set out from the beginning.

3   stopbullying.gov, "Facts about Bullying," Accessed Online, January 2020. https://www.stopbullying.gov/media/facts/index.html.

4   Erin Duffin, "Number of children living with a single mother or a single father in the U.S. from 1970 to 2019," Statista, January 2020. https://www.statista.com/statistics/252847/number-of-children-living-with-a-single-mother-or-single-father/.

5   Ibid

6   Darcel Rockett, "Kids are seeing porn sooner than adults think," *Chicago Tribune*, April 2018. https://www.njherald.com/lifestyle/20180408/kids-are-seeing-porn-sooner-than-adults-think.

When we cling to the Victorian notion of childhood innocence as taught to us through novels, movies, and fantasy, we absorb the message that life isn't hard until adulthood. That parents can be perfect protectors if they choose to be.

The message then, and still familiar now, was to *enjoy life while you're young and deal with the struggles later*. Unfortunately, this leaves our children without any training in how to accept and respond to challenges and leaves adults simply longing for a better time rather than facing what's been given to them. If and when we are faced with struggles in childhood, we look back with regret, believing that our time of pure joy unmarked by struggle was stolen from us. We weren't given what was culturally promised to us.

For the children of Puritans, it must have been a miserable existence to be forced out of play or imagination for fear of fierce punishment. But neither was it useful for the Victorians—and us—to retain the ideal of a childhood so wonderful that we're never prepared to transition into adulthood. This shock of reality is perhaps most evident in the millennial concept of "adulting."

Perhaps the criticism for this generation's challenges in coping with adulthood is unfair. After all, the very notion of an idyllic childhood has been transferred to us from books written by adult authors—typically men, who were quite removed from the upbringing of children at all—and not as a reflection of true experiences. The concept of a childhood meant to be protected and preserved was not meant to be prescriptive but as a sense of literary escapism from nineteenth-century authors who appeared to be *adulting*-averse themselves.

What the Puritans and Victorians both missed, and what can

still cripple millennials and their generational peers today, is the integration of both suffering and joy.

Yes, many of us have at least some idyllic memories of warm summer days and carefree play in childhood. But most of us also have some childhood stress or struggle that's worth recalling as well. Yet few of us were equipped to cope with those struggles in healthy ways. Many weren't taught how to respond to what life throws at us, leaving us mourning the loss of a childhood that never was.

Instead of pretending that children experience only joy and fun until the day they become adults, why not teach everyone to respond to challenges as they come? After all, life has happened to us from birth. We cannot be hidden from it. Unless we are equipped with the awareness of the paradox that is a coexistence of joy and suffering and given tools to respond to it, then we become increasingly disempowered, generation after generation.

Imagine how much different we might grow to be if we could see the innocence of childhood die, like the Victorian stories of old, without mourning its loss? What if we could celebrate the birth of a new creature who sees life through a lens of experience, not fading the hopes of youth but bolstering them? The new person, born of time and adversity, would become a hybrid of sorts, who enjoys the benefits of knowledge as well as the youthful optimism for better things to come. Suffering or struggle should not rob us of hope—not when we can grow through them into stronger, better equipped human beings.

By striving to retain the hope of childhood in the midst of our experiences, we're more likely to come out on the other side, still holding on to our faith, conviction, compassion, and hope for the future.

> Unless we are equipped with the awareness of the paradox that is a coexistence of joy and suffering and given tools to respond to it, then we become increasingly disempowered, generation after generation.

TIME WOUNDS ALL HEELS

Adulthood is not an event that comes upon us overnight. It's a journey over time and experience—and for some, that journey happens at a much younger age than any of us would like. We can almost map its trajectory in the shift in values and characteristics that we hold. We might call it maturation or simply becoming jaded, but certain virtues that are deemed childlike begin to give way if they aren't carefully protected.

These virtues that we see as childlike include unconditional love, kindness, and compassion. We see children as quick to forgive and emotionally recover. We see a natural optimism in them and a belief in themselves and the world.

Each of these qualities seems to be instinctual, just as much as a baby sea turtle knows to crawl straight from the egg to the ocean. Can you imagine a human baby being born, then hours later walking to the fridge to get a drink? As a parent of seven, I have to admit that sounds appealing. Indulge me for just a moment, but what if they could clean themselves up or use the bathroom as soon as they were born. Oh, the bliss! I have only recently come out of eighteen straight years of diaper changing—*every day* for eighteen years.

Instant physical maturity would be a game-changer, but nature chose otherwise with us humans. (Thanks, Mother Nature.) But instead of being born with physical capabilities, we're given emotional powers—virtues that, if nurtured, can prepare us to face the struggles to come.

My kids, like most others, learn at an early age that they find joy when they make others happy. If they can make us laugh, they'll repeat that action over and over again. They are sad when others are sad and comfort them in the ways that they have been comforted. There's nothing sweeter than a young child kissing the bump or bruise on another child's arm or knee, then hugging them and asking if they're okay.

There's a level of empathy and optimism inherent in young children, a quickness to move on from pain, and desire to help others along as well, that we think of as childlike even when we see it in adults. These virtues are a natural counter to the extreme vulnerability that humans are born with compared to the animal kingdom.

The idea of these naturally virtuous children suffering is difficult to process, which is undoubtedly why we're inclined to shelter them as much as possible, even from the knowledge of such pain. How could there be meaning in the level of trauma that some children so heartbreakingly endure?

Psychiatrist and Holocaust survivor Viktor Frankl explored this concept with a psychological framework called *dimensional ontology*. If we were to picture this concept in geometric terms, we might see a cylinder, a cone, and a globe—each of them clearly a different shape. But if we were to shine a light from above, each one would cast the same circular shadow.

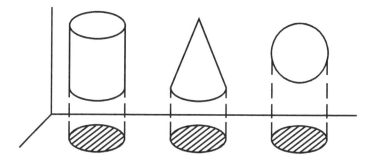

In a similar way, various circumstances can cast a shadow of pain and struggle that might all carry the same kind of painful symptomatology. There may not be a way to differentiate between them at first, just as it's difficult to identify the purpose of that pain in the moment. That's because we're experiencing it from the one or two dimensions of our present experience and character. It often isn't until the third dimension of time is introduced that we're able to gain some distance and perspective to gain a clearer understanding.

Meaning, then, is found on a higher plane than the one we're currently experiencing—thus the saying, *time heals all wounds.* When we accept that a reverse of sorts is true as well, that *time wounds all heels* and adversity comes to us all, we come to a greater sense of patience in our circumstances, waiting for the meaning to be revealed.

Everyone is going to face struggle as part of life, that it begins early, that we can choose how we respond to it, and that we will discover more of its value and application in time. In this light, suffering does not steal from us—it is our poor responses to suffering that chip away at our virtues.

THE APPRECIATION OF ALL THINGS

Of the tragic stories to come from the Holocaust, sisters Corrie and Betsie ten Boom stand out not only for their well-known plight in a concentration camp, but for their remarkable outlook on life, memorialized in Corrie's book *The Hiding Place*.

The sisters were devout Christian girls, imprisoned for harboring Jewish refugees in their home. As the story goes, the barracks in which they were confined were dimly lit, foul-smelling, flea-infested, crowded, and constantly patrolled by guards. They had one Bible that they were able to sneak in, and when they could, they would read to each other from it. On one occasion, Betsie read the phrase, "In everything, give thanks."

Corrie balked. "Everything? Even the fleas?"

Betsie replied, "Yes, Corrie. We should be thankful for everything. Even for the fleas."

Reluctantly, Corrie gave thanks for everything, as did her sister. It wasn't until later that they realized just why the fleas should be on that list. Betsie overheard a supervisor complaining about their cell—no one wanted to enter it because of the fleas, which gave the sisters some cherished privacy.

The only way the sisters could read their smuggled Bible and worship without further endangering their lives was if they endured the flea infestation. They were daily irritants that served a much greater purpose. I imagine it was much easier to be grateful for the fleas after that realization came to light.

There is another layer to consider here, however, and that is the difference between gratitude and appreciation. The word grateful comes from the Latin word *gratus*, which means *pleasing*—certainly not a term attributable to parasitic pests. Appreciation, on the other hand, is the act of estimating the quality or worth—*appretiare*—generally with the sense of a high value.

If we can begin to estimate the quality of our suffering, and perhaps over time begin to respond favorably to it as something of high value, our response begins to shift. The fleas were never pleasing or enjoyable, but they did become quite valuable to them as they sought spiritual and emotional sustenance.

This is where our agency lays in the midst of stress, strain, and difficulty: it is not in the conditions themselves, but in how we choose to respond to them.

STRESSORS BIG AND SMALL

We've spoken a great deal about suffering to this point, so much that trauma may seem to be the focus. This is not the full embodiment of personal growth, but a critical foundation to be laid. We must first emphasize, perhaps by stark contrast, how important it is for us to embrace hardship in order to become victorious in our struggles and achieve the much sought-after peace and joy. Suffering certainly makes the clearest connection to the pressure and darkness of being buried, and it is often the first thing that we turn our focus away from, allowing it to crush us. But not all struggle is so extreme. Stress is simply the byproduct of trying to control something that we, in fact, have no control over.

My CBT therapist would remind me that the goal isn't to

eliminate stress, but to manage it.[7] Just by trying to eliminate it, we're attempting to control what we cannot, thereby creating more stress. It's an avoidance of reality that seems to plague our culture.

Gallup's 2019 emotions report provided a snapshot of how we're doing, and it isn't great. More than 55 percent of Americans recalled feeling stress for *much of the day* in 2018. Nearly half felt worried, and more than a fifth felt angry.[8]

These numbers come in just below Greece, who topped the charts, but before the African nation of Chad, which is widely recognized as one of the world's most pain-stricken populations. Even scarier, these numbers were an increase from 2017. We are becoming more and more stressed over time, in spite of improved quality of life. With a burgeoning economy and near limitless resources at our societal fingertips, we're angrier than we've ever been before.

And these stressors are beginning to plague us younger and younger.

A study published in the journal *Social Indicators Research* took samplings across seven million people to monitor changes over time. As summarized for a San Diego State University publication:

Compared to their 1980s counterparts, teens in the 2010s are 38

---

7   CBT stands for Cognitive Behavioral Therapy and is one of many excellent resources available to help us accept and adapt to stressors big and small. I highly recommend professional help, especially if you can relate to the darker struggles we've discussed here. Don't wait seven years and for your spouse to drag you to the doctor.

8   Josh Hafner, "The misery is real: A third of the world is stressed, worried and in pain, Gallup report finds," *USA Today*, April 2019.

percent more likely to have trouble remembering, 74 percent more likely to have trouble sleeping and twice as likely to have seen a professional for mental health issues.

College students surveyed were 50 percent more likely to say they feel overwhelmed, and adults were more likely to say their sleep was restless, they had poor appetite and everything was an effort—all classic psychosomatic symptoms of depression.[9]

Some of the increase in these claims could be attributed to leaps in mental healthcare. When my mum and stepfather divorced in my teen years, I was taken to the doctor for suspected anemia. I was pale and lethargic, but all of my levels came back fine. When they asked what might be going on in my life, I explained that my mother and stepfather were going through a very unpleasant divorce. Now it was clear: "That's what it is, Ben. You're not anemic—you're depressed."

But understanding wasn't enough. I was sent home with an answer but no solutions. We did nothing at all.

If we're not experiencing mental health struggles more, we're understanding them better, allowing us to identify and talk about them more as well. But understanding is still only half the equation, and we've known Americans to be stressed out for some time now.

What is it that we're actually feeling buried beneath—and do those things matter in the long run? Are we getting caught up in the thick of thin things?

---

9   SDSU NewsCenter, "Americans Reporting Increased Symptoms of Depression," San Diego State University, September 2014. Accessed Online http://newscenter.sdsu.edu/sdsu_newscenter/news_story.aspx?sid=75201.

Stress is simply the byproduct of trying to control something that we, in fact, have no control over.

AWAKENING THE DORMANT SEEDS

At just twenty-one years old, working in graphic design, I learned to personally evaluate every step of the work I was part of. I would look at my goals and expectations from the onset, then evaluate what actually happened and how I could do better afterward.

As my career progressed, this practice has served me well as an entrepreneur, as well as in management, and as the global president of an international company in a multibillion-dollar industry. I've worked in graphic design, sales and marketing, training, senior management, and consultancy. I've been in start-ups, established markets, mature businesses, and sat on the board of directors for trade associations. In each of these environments, there's a nearly universal inclination to say, "If we just…"

If we just had a better handle on shipping time. *If we just* had a better price on production. *If we just* had this video or this tool or this website function. *If we just* had this one product. *If we just* responded quicker to this regulation or complaint.

The real missing piece, more than any individual action or process, is personal development. What's needed is introspection and analysis of ourselves, as much as study and analysis of a product or initiative.

People are the greatest asset any of us has in business, yet we expect to leave our private lives at home, ignoring how deeply our personal struggles affect how present and effective we can be at work. No matter how much we want to create a work environment free of personal stress, there is no way to truly leave who we are and what we're struggling with at the door. We might put on a mask of buoyancy and optimism for our clients and co-workers, but beneath it will be the same pain, emptiness, or stress weighing us down day to day. It'll eventually affect the way we view challenges in the workplace, respond to staff, and interact with customers and clients. The time taken to self-improve, or to allow space for improvement in our people, returns dividends in business that are priceless.

The reverse impact is also true: struggles at work will color our day to day outside the office. If you have a boss who is demanding and intimidating, or you've been knocked down over and over as an entrepreneur, those feelings of anxiety and vulnerability will feed into your emotional makeup and affect all aspects of your life. They'll change the belief you have in yourself to manage difficult things.

Similarly, when we grapple with our challenges directly and seek to grow from them, it can become a virtuous cycle for all aspects of our lives. Business informs personal and vice versa, and we learn to do better, be better, and grow into something more as a result.

Whether you're struggling with a chronic condition or are an entrepreneur, acknowledge and come to accept the truth that you're always going into or coming out of varying degrees of adversity. Just as a state of pure childhood innocence cannot be protected, stressors cannot be completely eliminated from any aspect of our adult lives. Even more frustratingly, the lessons we have to learn are rarely one-time events, for it's within the repetition that we continue to grow.

It's within the risk and the strain that we're stretched and pulled, constantly reminding us that we don't have all the answers. This is the necessity of being planted—covered up and pressed down by circumstances that will force us to grow.

Because understanding isn't enough, acknowledging the stress of recurring adversity is only helpful if we're ready to face it and respond. If we aren't open to the nourishing qualities of struggle, we will remain dormant and buried indefinitely. Therefore, it isn't enough to simply accept struggle, just as we cannot simply pursue joy.

On the other hand, making excuses for our circumstances or enmeshing ourselves with them is simply another aspect of avoidance—the same kind that plagued me for nearly a decade of silent struggle. Giving up and saying, "That's who I am" or "That's the lot I've been dealt" is like a seed that dissolves into compost instead of breaking forth into a sprout. The second we decide that we're always going to live this way—feeling buried, overwhelmed, and hopeless—we become disempowered. We deny ourselves the privilege of improvement.

By facing the reality of our circumstances with a desire for learning and personal growth, we become open to the lessons our unique circumstances have given us. Only then do we begin to feel the purpose of being planted, and the darkness is not so difficult to face.

CHANGING OUR PERSPECTIVE
OF ADVERSITY

The presence of stress is unpleasant, but consider that it is our response to difficult things that determines our potential and true possibilities. Here are some questions you might ask yourself for further exploration of the nature of adversity and your response to it.

- If we were to shed Victorian notions of complete innocence and deserved trial-free seasons, how might we view life differently? Have you really been robbed or put on the wrong path?
- How might your perspective change if you stopped referring to trials as unwanted or undeserved stress and simply faced them as they are?
- How are you currently facing your challenges? Do you acknowledge them? Accept them? How do you deal with them?
- How do you currently measure your ability to deal with stress or difficult things?
- What are some benefits that can be experienced as a consequence to your struggles if you respond well?

Chapter 2

EMERGING FROM THE DARKNESS

PARADOX: SOMETIMES WE MUST ENDURE THE CIRCUMSTANCES THAT WE MOST WANT TO AVOID

As a seed interacts with the soil around it, the hard, outer shell begins to break down to let more nutrients in. The first signs of a root then emerges, digging down into the ground to anchor the plant and draw even more out of the soil. Next comes a tiny shoot, making its way through the ground in search of the warmth of the sun.

There is no shortage of commentary on nature's metaphors for personal growth. From the seed's undoing to the restorative work of a forest fire, everything in the plant and animal kingdom is built to survive, adapting to its circumstances to preserve life at all costs. Alongside the tiny seed growing into a sturdy, fruit-bearing tree, one of the best of these metaphors for personal change is the butterfly.

Butterflies grace everything from classic children's books to ancient Greek symbolism. Humanity has long been fascinated with the mystery of the caterpillar's miraculous transformation. Yet we don't often talk about just how that process works. It's easiest to think of it in terms of addition, the caterpillar somehow growing wings from its body. There's a struggle within the chrysalis,[10] but all we see is the caterpillar emerging victorious as a beautiful butterfly.

However, beneath the protective layers of the chrysalis, there is something much more significant happening than growth alone. The caterpillar doesn't slowly grow from one state to the other, as we can observe in a tadpole growing into a frog. The caterpillar is completely lost, replaced by something beautiful that has been forged in loss, struggle, and potentially pain.[11]

The loss of the caterpillar is full: inside the chrysalis, dormant genes within the caterpillar are activated, which then begin to dissolve its own tissue into a genetic soup. Then that free-floating material that was once a caterpillar begins to recreate itself into something new entirely.

For the butterfly to remake itself, the caterpillar must be completely undone.

Each of us has experienced something similar in our lives. Though no two of our "chrysalises" are alike, there is something activated within us once the struggle begins. Once we have received knowledge, experience, struggle, or suffering in some way, it undoes us. We can't return to that place of blissful ignorance again, but we do have a choice that the butterfly

---

10   https://mitchteemley.com/2015/01/06/caterpillars-dont-become-butterflies/.

11   Truthfully, we don't know yet whether insects feel pain, but for the purposes of the metaphor, a time of undoing is certainly unpleasant.

does not: will we remain undone, or fight to emerge with new beauty and power?

The ideal of innocence is difficult to let go of until we look closer at the definition of the word. The root comes from an old French word, *in nocere*, meaning "to not hurt."[12] This could be thought of as the way that a little child hasn't yet hurt anyone, embodying the guiltless, blameless, and harmless associations of innocence; or the way that we think of children as unharmed themselves, not yet touched by the challenges of life. Naïve, unknowing, and inexperienced.

I cannot say what the caterpillar feels as it dissolves into liquid, and I don't think a seed feels anything as its protective layers give way for the sprout to emerge—but I do know that the process isn't pleasant for us. Therein lies another paradox of empowerment, because it's in our nature to resist pain in spite of the fact that we need it for our progress. We are hardwired with survival mechanisms that send us running, resisting, or refusing to move until the danger has passed. Yet we're also gifted with ambition—a desire to explore, discover, and push the limits. The battle between self-preservation and self-authoring rages on, and the longer we refuse the transformation, the more prolonged that discomfort will be.

As we mature and allow experience to replace innocence, we become something new. We're no longer the romanticized child, and it's up to us whether we remain undone or continue the work of re-creation. Without intentionality, many of us spend years as miserly, pessimistic adults just trying to get on with

---

12   Doris Bühler-Niederberger, "Innocence and Childhood," Oxford Bibliographies. Last Reviewed April 2017. https://www.oxfordbibliographies.com/view/document/obo-9780199791231/obo-9780199791231-0161.xml.

our lives. What a waste of experience that is, for the butterfly is more beautiful and more capable than the caterpillar can ever be. The tree is more prolific and stronger than a seed can ever be.

Whatever your chrysalis might be, there is great value in submitting to the undoing that it has activated. Unpleasant though it may be, there is greatness on the other side. With time, patience, and humility, you will one day emerge from the darkness into the warmth of the sun as a new creature with wings to fly to greater heights.

> We hope more, believe and become more, not in spite of the struggle, but because of it.

HONORING THE TRANSFORMATION

As a young professional, I became the general manager of two markets for a global, multibillion-dollar consumer goods company. I'll explain how that happened in the next chapter. For now, a specific incident comes to mind that transformed me from a young, uncertain newcomer in the industry, to someone with great experience and confidence because of it.

It was January, just a couple of years since I'd been hired, and we were just gearing up for a great new year, ready to achieve all that our business plans and budgets had prepared us for. We had goals and targets and teams all lined up, excited to start a new year with new aspirations. During my trip to a global communications conference in Munich, Germany, a phone call changed everything.

The call came from my external affairs manager, who was fielding an emergency, and I was pulled from the middle of a session to take her call. She sounded panicked and clearly distressed as she relayed the bad news to me: "Representatives from the Department of Trade and Industry are here, and they have intent to take us to court and shut us down."

The Department of Trade and Industry was a government-based consumer protection organization that had obtained the right to ask us for any piece of information they wanted. We were obligated to comply without any idea what the charges were for or why they would need the information. They gave us no more information than they had to: they intended to shut us down, they had a list of items they wanted, and they were going to set up camp in our offices until they got it.

All of our goals and aspirations for the year were suddenly shelved. They were quite literally in our faces every single day, with agents working from within our offices and refusing to be ignored. They became the chrysalis that signaled our undoing, wrapping us up in a crisis of overwhelming proportion.

For almost a year, we hosted a group of forensic accountants, which is a role I hadn't even heard of before then. They came and went in and out of our office as they pleased, demanding data and documentation and interrupting our work at will—all with the very real threat of court looming over our heads. Like the forensic scientists that CSI-type television shows have made us all familiar with, these officials used their forensic attention to dig into the details of a company and draw conclusions that affected their case. They were intelligent, lightning-fast, and laser-focused on their agenda.

Their department had a success rate of more than 90 percent

when they went after a company, and many businesses went bankrupt before even getting to defend themselves against the charges due to the immediate impact they would have on running the business. There was great risk in fighting the charges, but perhaps more in letting the case unfold on its own. Our office was inconvenienced during that year of investigation, but the local market's tens of millions in turnover, as well as the global corporation's billions were all at risk if we did nothing.

> For the butterfly to form, the caterpillar must be completely undone.

Our deep pockets and thriving global presence meant we had an advantage over the others that they'd gone after. Eventually, when we determined that it was the business model itself that they were after, it meant the threat impacted our entire industry. Not only did we have the resources to stand up for ourselves, but we had an obligation to try on behalf of others too.

This required our business model be transformed into something better. In many ways, we had to create something brand new that resolved the concerns that were coming to light, all while operating under the nose of investigators.

Together with a crisis team created from all levels of experience within the company and outside of it, my executive team and I formed a response plan and got to work. We retained experts on all levels—local, European, and global. We had experts on investigations, similar court cases, and industry law. We also brought in communication experts, marketing consultations, business managers, and executives to help us keep the business moving while the case was underway.

It was fierce, enduring, and a challenge I couldn't have foreseen in my brief time on the job.

In response, we left no stone unturned. Some of the concerns that came to light were legitimate problems that we needed to address. Others were misunderstandings that needed clarifying and standing up for. Over time, we could identify their concerns by the nature of their questions and the information they kept circling around. Some of those changes affected the entire industry, which was watching closely to see how we would respond. Our job was to fix what was broken, protect what wasn't, and move forward stronger as a result.

On the other side of it all, we made changes that were for the good of the business and the industry as a whole—and we also proved our accusers wrong in many cases. Their intention to shut us down did not prevail. We bent the law of averages to our good, won the court case, and set standards for our industry that I remain proud of to this day. However, my innocence in that business was lost. And that's okay!

Before the crisis, I was thrilled to be managing the company at such a young age, but it colored the way I viewed myself in the role. My age was always a factor. If someone with seniority told me something, I took it as the final word. I was surrounded by people with more than a decade in the company and extensive experience in the industry. I accepted tenure, age, and loyalty as stand-ins for accuracy. In my mind, everything they taught me had to be completely true.

When those supposed truths were challenged by forensic accountants, everything came into question. During the process, it felt like an upheaval, but the benefit of comparison opened my eyes. Instead of one voice of authority with one message, I now had two: devoted and loyal colleagues, and negative and hostile agents.

If I had kept the same deference for my company that informed my early years in that role, it would have been difficult or impossible to challenge our business model in response to the investigation.

Plenty of voices told me to go a different direction—one that was more popular, more convenient, or more in line with tradition and culture. But what was convenient wasn't necessarily right. The culture and tradition and popular consensus needed to change if we wanted to win. It was an uphill fight that left me unpopular on many sides for a time.

Just as I had to learn with my health, I was reminded that accepting the struggle isn't about giving in—it's about facing reality and then fighting with everything you've got in order to win.

SEASONS OF LOSS AND NEW GROWTH

Cycles of darkness, struggle, and loss are not simply part of life, but necessary for it. The caterpillar emerges, night gives way to day, winter gives way to spring. It's more than a cycle of individual events. We more fully appreciate the day because of the night, not in spite of it. We need the depths of winter in order to appreciate the fullness of spring.

Even the most extreme sense of loss—the burning of a forest—clears the way for new, healthy growth. As with so many things, nature mirrors our experiences. We will cycle through moments of darkness and seasons of winter, each moment carrying its own purpose. Occasionally we need a forest fire to burn away the extraneous and strengthen what should remain.

That particular crisis was a forest fire. For the business, it burned away the models and thinking that were keeping us back. It did a number on my own life as well. It burned down my insecurities, my lack of conviction. It made way for the new growth of confidence and assertiveness. As I moved along in that company and in future roles, my experience lent confidence to others, and as they asked my opinion and sought my expertise, that new growth was nurtured and fed. Over the course of that year, I blossomed into a stronger leader.

The pressure, isolation, and darkness of that experience were intense, but I was able to draw from what had been given to me and eventually break forth as a new person, new manager, and new leader.

It gave me insight and perspective that I couldn't have learned from university or from mentors. It caused me to dig deep enough to understand what the business was truly about, what problems we needed to solve, and what was right and wrong within our culture. It caused me to form genuine opinions based on fact and substance, not handed-down traditions. It taught me to take control of the situation and respond decisively.

None of my hopes for that company included such a major upheaval, but few of our childlike aspirations do come to fruition. Sometimes we lose sight of them, but more often, they collapse because they were never built on a solid foundation. They're wishes that we hope will come true. Instead, over time and with experience, our goal is to cultivate the hope that fueled those wishes so it can encourage wiser, more realistic dreams.

A child who wants to be an astronaut is making a wish, but a child who grows up studying sciences, then goes to university and masters the classes, then stays on top of their game physically and mentally is no longer making a wish. Now they are pursuing a future with confidence and hope.

With each struggle, my confidence for the future becomes stronger than ever before. Coming through that ordeal became a resume talking point for the rest of my career. Most of my interviews include a conversation about that court case and the insights and experience I gleaned from it. Instead of childlike excitement and fears about inexperience, I could confidently relay my actions and how the lesson I learned might apply in the new role.

In other words, we hope more and believe more not in spite of the struggle, but because of it.

So let the fires come. Let them burn away naiveté, impatience, and impulsiveness. Let them destroy ignorance and innocence. The loss will always be replaced by new shoots of virtue and strength, as long as we continue to cultivate that growth in our lives.

THE BRIGHT SIDE OF STRESS

In Greek mythology, Sisyphus was infamous for his trickery, twice cheating death. His final comeuppance came in the form of an eternal punishment: he was confined to a hill in the depths of the Underworld, condemned to roll a boulder from the bottom to the top. But every time he reached the top, the boulder would roll back to the bottom. This was his task, every day, for all eternity.

Our Sisyphean task—one of little value that we are doomed to repeat indefinitely—comes when we refuse to surrender to the circumstances that life has brought to us. Day after day, we go through the motions of life, holding the struggle on our shoulders. Yet it is not the gods condemning us to repeat the task, but our own choice to let go of the lessons and lose the boulder.

Sometimes, it is our childlike desire to avoid pain and distress that makes us miss the opportunity locked within the struggle. On a very basic level, the stress response alerting us to danger that we must avoid has saved the human race. It has helped us to fight and to flee in order to preserve ourselves, generation after generation.

In 1974, Hungarian endocrinologist Hans Selye identified the difference between the kind of stress that we should avoid, and what he called *eustress*, with *eu* being the Greek prefix for "good." Long before that, Chinese lettering combined the characters for *danger* and *opportunity* to form the word *stress*. It is truly a paradoxical state, in which there is opportunity for growth that we should pursue, as well as a risk of danger that we must avoid.

In a 2003 study, LeFevre, Matheny, and Kolt described our perception of the challenges of life as much less nuanced: "Stress has become a synonym for distress, a state of ill-being in which happiness and comfort have been surrendered."[13]

---

13   Juliette Tocino-Smith, Msc, "What is Eustress And How is It Different than Stress?" PositivePsychology.com, October 2019. https://positivepsychology.com/what-is-eustress/.

It is true that negative stress, which we'll differentiate here as distress, is a health risk—a physical knock to the body that comes as a consequence of prolonged anxieties. I watched this happen with my father when, the night before his own court case, he experienced a significant heart attack. The distress of what was coming triggered a physical response that nearly killed him.

Eustress, the positive kind of stress, also changes us on a biological level, signaling an increase in hormones that bring up heart rate and blood pressure, plunging the brain into a state of hyperawareness encased with emotional calm and physical relaxation.

SELYE'S SIGNS OF EUSTRESS	SELYE'S SIGNS OF DISTRESS
Short-term	Short-term as well as long-term
Energizes and motivates	Can trigger anxiety, concern, and unpleasant feelings
Perceived as within our ability to cope	Perceived as surpassing our ability to cope
Increases focus and performance	Decreases focus and performance
Helps to develop and support the fight-or-flight mechanism	Contributes to physical and mental challenges

Eustress might be experienced when starting a new romantic relationship, getting married, starting a new job, buying a home, traveling, going on holiday, having a child, or exercising. Any of those environments could also be distressing, based on personality and circumstance, because any degree of meaningful change brings with it an element of stress. The key difference between the perceptions of stress lies in the way we feel able to cope. Even situational eustress can tip the scales into distress once we can no longer cope. In that instance, the same increases in heart rate and focus that can be a benefit to us in the short-term will quickly become a threat.

If we can begin to face our challenges without wallowing in them, we become much more empowered to move beyond them, ready for what's to come. Or at least, as ready as we can be.

WAITING FOR THE LIGHT

Not all struggles last for a night. Some endure for great lengths of time. Some are cold but expected seasons, while others rage and burn unpredictably and uncontrollably. Such was the case when my oldest child, Ethan, developed a kidney disorder at the age of three.

Within the space of about four days, my tiny little boy put on half of his body weight in water retention. At the hospital, he was diagnosed with nephrotic syndrome and was treated with vast amounts of steroids.

There's something heart-wrenching about going to a hospital at all, let alone for a little child. During our first stay, Kim was pregnant with our third child and struggling to walk long distances due to an issue with her pelvis. When she came to visit, I would carry our son down to meet her at the front door, then lay him in her lap and push the two of them in a wheelchair back up to the room. All along the corridors, visible expressions of sympathy were directed not at her in the wheelchair, but the visibly sick little boy in her lap. We were the family that no one wants to be.

The medication healed and protected his kidneys as planned,

but they also knocked out his immune system. Then he would get sick, which put a strain on his kidneys, which triggered a relapse, which required more steroids. For weeks, Ethan was dosed up on steroids until he finally stabilized enough to go home.

One of our instructions for his care was to make sure he didn't get chickenpox. In his weakened state, the inflammation from that particular disease could travel to the brain and cause lethal or at least life-changing damage.

You probably have guessed, but just a few weeks after this admonishment from the doctors, he did, in fact, come down with chickenpox. This time, his multi-week stay in the hospital had the added layer of isolation in order to avoid him being exposed to anything at all.

Imagine a typical three-year-old, hooked up to a drip and isolated from the rest of the world, still needing to be entertained and happy while also being puffed up and not feeling well. Every day was a challenge, but one day in particular was traumatic for us all.

The first time the hospital staff put a cannula in his hand, he was innocent as to what was coming. Unaffected by the trial, he let them proceed without a problem. He didn't know to be afraid. But the second time, he wasn't having any of it. I watched as my firstborn little son thrashed around on the bed, terrified of what was to come, helpless to make it better for him, until the nurses asked me to hold him down.

Reluctantly, I joined him on the hospital bed, wrapping him up so that he couldn't move his arm. As we lay there together, my terrified and crying little boy called out to me, "Daddy, they're hurting me. Why are you letting them hurt me?"

It took three tries to get the cannula in, including an attempt that bent one needle in his hand. Kim and I took turns holding him down so that, from his perspective and in spite of anything we could do to help him understand, strangers could hurt him over and over again. It was too much. And yet, we continued on, because we knew what he didn't: a little bit of pain now would prevent a lot of pain later.

WHEN THE TRIALS ARE TOO MUCH TO BEAR

It would take another two years of hospital visits, checks with consultants, and daily checks for protein output before my son would get better. We're incredibly blessed that he did at all. Many families have different stories that do not end as well.

When distress reaches all-consuming proportions such as those, the only way to cope with it is to take one moment at a time. If we try to project ourselves out into a future where all we can see is pain, it becomes too much to bear. But by managing what we can in each moment—and nothing more than that—we can keep moving forward, however slowly.

I couldn't eliminate nephrotic syndrome for Ethan, but I could hold him through his distress. I could support the doctors as they managed his symptoms. I could support my wife when it was her turn at the hospital. I could rely on her, my other children, my parents, my in-laws, and the doctors to each manage what was in their control. I could trust them enough to feel supported when I became overwhelmed. None of us were alone.

When we feel diminished, contracting under the pressure of our circumstances, others have room to expand. As the love and strength of others begin to wrap around us and lift us up, we are better able to cope. Feeling loved and valued even when we have nothing to give allows us to recognize the importance of this part of the journey. One day, we'll be able to repay the favor, expanding for someone who needs us.

This expansion and contraction, an ever-shifting give-and-take, moves between us all like the collective breath of humanity. Each exchange gets us through another moment, another day, another season, bringing us all one step closer to the light.

THE PURSUIT OF SELF-POSSESSION

As we saw in the last chapter, each season of life is meant to be accepted for what it has to offer. When we come to terms with that reality, we are better able to endure with patience and hope for a stronger future. As we'll see in the next chapter, humility is vital in making way for new shoots of personal growth hidden behind our doubts and limiting beliefs.

However, we must also acknowledge that this is a constant practice that can never be perfected. Even the sturdiest trees can be threatened by strong winds, heavy snows, and fires. Even when we grow beyond the feeling of being buried and dormant, we will always remain rooted into that same soil that helped us to emerge.

If the soil of adversity is what feeds us, the forces that threaten to uproot us are such that can loosen our grip on present circumstances and the value that they bring.

To be self-possessed in these times is not the same as having full control. The world teaches us that we can have it all, do it all, be it all, but it's simply not true. There is no way to be in perfect control of all areas of life—health, finances, reputation, employment, economy, weather. Something will always slip through our grasp. At most, we might only have influence on what befalls us in a given moment.

What we do have, however, is control of our response.

To be self-possessed is to control what is ours and nothing more. It is to let go of the expectation that we have to cope by ourselves, or the limiting self-belief that stress is a sign of our inadequacies.

As we emerge from the soil of adversity, finally accepting our challenge to learn and grow from life's challenges, the next step is to accept the fragile state that we're in as part of humanity. We can accept our weaknesses as part of who we are, and take responsibility for where we can grow and overcome. We can look at ourselves with a new sense of responsibility, appreciation, and respect. We can become the kind of person who knows where we're going, how to get there, how to manage ourselves, and, when in leadership, how to manage others as well.

NURTURING A PATIENT SENSE
OF ENDURANCE

The next time you're feeling the effects of stress, burnout, or trauma, consider whether your self-preservation or self-authoring instincts are taking over.

- Are you looking toward the pain or away from it?
- Are there areas of your life that you are trying to control that are not yours to control?
- If you are struggling with major adversity, can you identify the people in your life that are expanding in your life in the form of added support?
- As you focus on the present, what lessons or insights are you learning from your adversity that is feeding your future self?

Chapter 3

SAPLINGS IN THE ELEMENTS

PARADOX: OUR GREATEST
INDIVIDUAL STRENGTH IS FOUND
IN OUR INTERCONNECTEDNESS

There are times when self-possession—controlling what is ours and acting only on what we can change—feels like too much. You don't have to look far for examples. If not you, then someone around you is feeling overwhelmed at this very moment. It happens at every level of every major corporation and in every small business, start-up, and family. Perhaps it's a demanding work schedule or employer that makes your work/life balance feel out of control. Or growing expectations and unforeseen lessons of leadership are rising with magnificent complexity. Maybe the loss of a loved one causes such grief that it seems your hurt will never heal. Maybe it's the books at home that won't balance or the mortgage that has become difficult to meet. Storms of overwhelm come to all of us at some point, but what is important is the assurance that we can weather them and keep moving forward. Like a sapling tree, our best chance of remaining rooted is by latching ourselves to an external source of support.

A number of years ago, while leading a small group within a general addiction recovery program, a disheveled, slightly inebriated woman shuffled in with a friend. Her head was so sunken into her shoulders, weighed down by obvious shame and self-loathing that it was almost buried into the cavity of her chest. Her eyes were glazed with alcohol and grief, and her puffy, reddened cheeks were stained with tears. She was more visibly broken and uncomfortable in her own skin than anyone I'd witnessed before or since. She was clearly in need of help, but the rules of the group were clear: the alcohol in her system meant I had to ask her to leave.

She lived just up the street, but I had never seen her come to a meeting before. I'm not sure what brought her in that night other than the fact that she desperately needed what we had to offer.

I put my arm around her shoulder, noticing with great pain the scars lining her forearms and wrists, and broke the news to her as delicately as I could.

"I really want to have you here, but you're not going to get the best out of it with alcohol in your system, and it won't be helpful for the others in the room either. The best thing that you can do is to go home, sleep it off, and come back with a clean system and a fresh mind. But until then, I need to ask you to head home."

She nodded, with fresh tears rolling down her face, and agreed.

I continued, striving to offer some encouragement and support: "Just promise me you'll be back. Our next meeting is on Wednesday at seven o'clock. Promise me you'll come back to that meeting."

This time, the woman shook her head.

It wasn't a lack of interest or commitment that she expressed, but a lack of self-belief. It was too many broken promises in the past to be able to make one more. It was being so broken herself that she didn't know if she could walk to another hour-long meeting for the sake of saving her own life.

She couldn't make me any promises. She couldn't make anyone promises anymore.

Almost immediately, I realized the error in my thinking. "I'm sorry," I told her. "I've got that back to front. Instead, let *me* make a promise to *you*: every Wednesday night at seven o'clock, regardless of what's going on, we are here for you. It doesn't matter if it's Christmas. We'll be here."

The next week, we saw her again, sober, and ready for the meeting. Not because her belief in herself had suddenly changed, but because she knew someone else cared for her.

Often, the starting point for developing the belief that we can make it through the tough stuff is the knowledge that someone cares for us and believes in us. That encouragement fills the void that our own lack of belief or conviction creates.

Paradoxically, it is by developing positive beliefs that we begin to see and prevent the limiting beliefs that stop us from growing. The more developed our character, the more control we have over our emotions, and the greater our sense of self-worth will be. When we value ourselves fully, our beliefs continue their positive trajectory, fueling continued growth.

When we become more patient, kind, forgiving, committed, driven, and educated, our view of the world and ourselves becomes clearer. Life becomes better, we become stronger, and positive beliefs are reinforced. Focusing only on our weaknesses and inadequacies has an opposite effect, triggering the spiral down to the proverbial and dreaded "rock bottom."

As I promised in the introduction, I don't believe this lowest of lows is a necessary evil—not when we can identify the spiral before it's too late and step outside of ourselves to draw support and belief from the collective of humanity. For it is through connection that we find our greatest strength.

> It's not about how important we can become, it's about what difference we can make. And we can't make a meaningful difference if we are preoccupied with living for ourselves.

THE STRENGTH OF HUMILITY

There is a paradox in self-worth and humility—the two virtues being intrinsically related: we are both nothing and everything at once. An infant left alone, independent of its parents' love and support, would die within days. In the sense that they have no way to fend for themselves and ensure their own survival, they are nothing. Yet to the parents, that infant is everything. The child's life is of greater worth to the parents than their own, creating an emotional connection that spurs us to care for their every need.

Though our independence grows with time, the paradox continues with the great half-truth so many people feel: that we're not enough.

It's partly true, certainly, that by ourselves we're like little children separated from our parents. But like little children, we are also loved and have worth in spite of our shortcomings.

Humility is a recognition of the whole truth, which is that we are everything and nothing simultaneously. We are a valuable part of the collective of humanity, neither an irrelevant part nor the sum of it as a whole, and our part makes a very real difference.

We can choose empowering beliefs and reach out for the support of others from a place of humility. In contrast, limiting beliefs are often isolating and self-centric. Humility is power, not passivity. It is how we become free of the obligation to be everything at all times, because we always have more to learn, and we always have more resources to draw from. True humility is a constant reminder of our greater self-worth due to our interconnected role within the whole of mankind.

POWER IN THE COLLECTIVE

Each of us is woven into the fabric of a family, a group of friends, a community, a society, and the world. As a collective, we are strong enough, big enough, and powerful enough to deal with whatever is thrown our way.

Yet we don't always experience the true power of this interconnectedness. Too often, we sever ourselves from others when we struggle and become isolated in our adversity. The connectedness that we feel will certainly vary with significance and in various stages of life. But consider for a moment that the vastness of 7.8 billion people and their collective resources, knowledge, experience, history, and loving kindness means that you have far more at your disposal than you give yourself credit for.

You don't need to know everyone on the planet to tap into these resources, either. Maybe you just need to make a new friend or reach out to someone in the office and ask for help with the project you're struggling with or open up to your spouse, child, parent, or significant other a little more. What's more, this isn't something we should simply consider as a nice idea. It is something we need to do in order to thrive in this life.

I don't mean this to be aspirational, though it is, of course, a lovely thought. I mean it quite literally. The fact is that we are directly and physiologically impacted by our interactions with others.

In one study, three or more incidents of intense stress within a year tripled the death rate in socially isolated, middle-aged men, but had no impact on the death rate of men with many close relationships.[14] In another, researchers in intensive care units found the comforting presence of another person lowered blood pressure and slowed secretion of fatty acids that block arteries.[15] This means your heart is literally protected by your loved ones—in fact, heart rates themselves have been shown to synch up for people in close communication.[16]

Our bodies are designed to deliberately let other people change

---

14 Drucker, Christensen, and Goleman, *HBR's 10 Must Reads: On Managing Yourself*, Harvard Business Review Press, January 2011.

15 Ibid

16 Perhaps this is why the heart has historically been the metaphor that we use for love—this is literally where our bodies are affected by it.

us. There's an emotional reciprocity that takes place between two people, whether you're the one helping or in need of support.

We expect to feel negative emotions change the body—restlessness or sleeplessness, a racing mind and loss of energy, a change in appetite—but we often miss just how much our connection with others creates positive reactions as well.

We are directly and physiologically impacted by our interactions with others.

Daniel Goleman, one of the leading experts in emotional intelligence, describes just how thoroughly we respond to connection with his exploration of the brain. In his book *Emotional Intelligence*, he identifies all of the self-regulating systems in our body as closed-loop systems.[17] For example, our circulatory system can operate within itself, informed and regulated by processes within the body and no external stimulus. Although it can be impacted by something external, such as the constriction of a vein by a tourniquet, it does not require that feedback in order to function.

The emotional system, which is controlled in the limbic section of the brain, has an open loop. It not only uses but *requires* connections with other people in order to determine our feelings and moods, which then go on to affect the function of other systems in the body.[18]

---

17 Daniel Goleman, *Emotional Intelligence: Why It Can Matter More Than IQ*, Bantam, January 2012.

18 Bruce P. Doré, et al, "Helping Others Regulate Emotion Predicts Increased Regulation of One's Own Emotions and Decreased Symptoms of Depression," *Personality and Psychology Bulletin*, March 2017. http://journals.sagepub.com/doi/abs/10.1177/0146167217695558.

At a very basic level, this ensures the future of the human race.

If my limbic, emotional system were closed, I would be entirely unaffected by the cries of my children. But because we respond to the connections of others, I am immediately affected by their distress. Their distress signals trigger an emotional rescue response that enables us to soothe them and intuit their needs. My children's ages currently range from nineteen down to three, which means I have essentially had multiple toddlers in my home for nearly twenty years—waking up in the middle of the night, throwing up on the carpet, cutting their own hair, crying because I gave them exactly what they asked for and wanting *Peppa Pig*, *The Wiggles* or *Barney* on again and again and again. Yes, I have been triggered many times with this wonderful open loop system. And I repeatedly assure myself it is a blessing.

What we see here, though, is that we are constantly giving and receiving feedback with the people around us, drawing on their emotions and sharing our own. It's no wonder, then, that the act of service brings an emotional strength that few other tasks in life can accomplish.

I recall this experience surprising me when I was a teenager. A church leader asked a couple of my friends and me to visit a few elderly ladies who couldn't make it to church on Sundays. What started out as an obligation quickly became a couple of hours of chitchat, which turned into a regular part of my Sunday afternoon.

One of the ladies, Rita Connor, became a good friend of mine. I was eighteen and she was eighty, yet I looked forward to each of our visits. After every visit, my day was uplifted, and that became a great start to my week. Over time, if I had a stressful week with work or school or life, my first thought was to visit Rita.

She'd beam and tell me how thoughtful I was, but those visits were just as much for me as they were for her. Sometimes we would make small talk about the week, and other times she would bend my ear with stories from her youth. After an hour or so, I would have to get back to life, and we would say goodbye, both feeling uplifted.

There was no better way to learn the lesson of Saint Francis of Assisi: It is in giving that we receive.

THE IMPACT OF INTENT

I do want to acknowledge here that the feeling of overwhelm often makes the effort of human connection feel impossible. When I'm feeling especially stressed, adding one more thing to my schedule is just too much. Someone telling me to "go out and do good" would immediately frustrate me.

But be reassured: the simple thought of doing good is enough to change our brain chemistry.

Psychologist Marianna Pogosyan wrote this in *Psychology Today*:

> "Research has found many examples of how doing good in ways big or small not only feels good, but also does us good. For instance, the well-being-boosting and depression-lowering benefits of volunteering have been repeatedly documented, as has the sense of meaning and purpose that often accommodates altruistic behavior."[19]

---

19 Marianna Pogosyan PhD, "In Helping Others, You Help Yourself," *Psychology Today*, May 2018. https://www.psychologytoday.com/us/blog/between-cultures/201805/in-helping-others-you-help-yourself.

We find meaning, then, not only in our own suffering, but in service to others. The two go hand in hand, with one as a comforting balm to the other. In a practical sense, service can be as tangible as reaching out and as simple as making a donation. Pogosyan continues:

> "Even when it comes to money, spending it on others predicts an increase in happiness compared to spending it on ourselves. Moreover, there is now neural evidence from FMRI studies suggesting a link between generosity and happiness in the brain. For example, donating money to charitable organizations activates the same mesolimbic regions of the brain that respond to monetary rewards or sex. In fact, the mere intent and commitment to generosity can stimulate neural change and make people happier."[20]

Isn't it a relief to know that it only takes a thought? If we're stuck, depressed, stressed, anxious, discouraged, or disheartened, just the thought of being generous or kind in some way, at some point, brings an immediate benefit to our bodies and lifts ours spirits.

Thus, we find that humility gives us strength to reach out for help when we need it and cuts the ties of isolation we bind ourselves with. It also means that knowing that someone else loves us and believes in us can be an enabling power to take that step. Additionally, reaching out to lift others will, in turn, raise us up, not just when we take action, but in the very moment of inspiration to do so.

As we serve others and flex our new emotional muscles, we gain strength and ability beyond what we previously had. We become something more.

---

20 Ibid.

OUR PRIORITIES

I have learned that the frustration of being too busy to serve is often a signal that I need to reprioritize. To properly look after ourselves, we need to honestly evaluate what's on our plate. If any time at all has been given to destructive behaviors, then there is room to replace them and do some good instead.

Interestingly, the word *priority* means *the first* or *prior thing*. It's meant to be a singular word, denoting a singular experience. You cannot have multiple first or prior things—but that doesn't stop us from trying. We fill our schedules with so many things that we feel are important until nothing gets the full attention that it needs. Sometimes we even engage in prolonged destructive behaviors in an effort to self-medicate, such as scrolling aimlessly for hours on social media or wallowing in front of Netflix with a tub of ice cream. Just know that whatever we've kicked down the road in a Netflix binge is going to come back to be dealt with later.

If I were to make an argument for one true priority, it would be this: *take time to connect with someone else in a giving spirit. Build some self-care into your schedule, or you'll snap.* You'll find that your capacity to work more efficiently on your next priority, and the one after that, will be enriched.

UNMASKING IMPOSTER SYNDROME

Over the trajectory of my career, I have thrown myself into the deep end time and again, and time and again, I've found that

I can swim. By this, I mean the roles that I've applied for or even asked for outright were not 100 percent within my skill set, yet I've won the jobs or thrived in the roles regardless. I was certainly out of my depth when I started dating my wife, but that's a story for another day.

Every time a new opportunity presents itself, I'm scared. Before one interview, in particular, I believed I was significantly unqualified—but the potential for my life and career was too good to pass up. So I went for it.

Leading up to the interview, my wife helped me to prepare. We thought of questions that an interviewer might ask, then wrote them down with an answer for each. Every night for about two weeks, we pulled out our lists and rehearsed. She'd ask me the questions back to front and front to back, in sequence and out of it. Then I would ask her the questions as well, putting myself in the shoes of the interviewer to see if there were any other questions I might need to practice.

When it came time for the interview, I felt as prepared as anyone could. But there was something that I couldn't account for with practice: I was very young. Not only was I young, but I'm not a very tall man—think Bruno Mars, but nowhere near as cool—and I had something of a baby face at the time. It was a big position, and I looked like a little kid! That concern was going to stand out like the (very young) elephant in the room.

I had prepared for about 95 percent of the questions they asked me, and I gave excellent answers in return. I had statistics and handouts that anticipated their questions and even had quotes from their founders memorized—I nailed it.

When my wife picked me up afterward, I looked slightly panicked. She was concerned that it didn't go well. I told her, "No, it went great. I think they're going to invite me back for the second interview."

She was confused. "Isn't that good?"

"Yes, but now I have a new concern: I had just been enjoying the fantasy of it. Am I really good enough to get the job?"

The second interview took place at their European head office, located on sprawling premises in Munich, Germany. There were hundreds of staff in the building, and I was meeting with the most senior executives of a billion-dollar region of a multibillion-dollar company. Again, I was this baby-faced, little kid looking man-child in my eyes, waiting for my turn to interview.

The stress started to mount. *Maybe it's not a good decision. I should just be comfortable at home instead of out here feeling anxious. Maybe my ambition got the better of me.*

But again, the interview went really well, and again, they asked if I had any questions for them.

In the first interview, I had asked if my age was a concern. It was at the beginning of the interview, but not by the end. This time, I had another thought. I leaned forward in my seat, looked the interviewer in the eyes, and asked, "Is there anything that I've said or done in this interview that would give you any reason not to give me the job?"

The company's European president, who had asked me the

question, got a gleam in his eye. It was a cheeky question, but he was clearly glad that I asked it.

He told me something about internal candidates and matters of politics, then offered me a piece of advice: "Should you be successful in getting this job, some people in the office might not be running at the same pace that you are. Take the first six months as a honeymoon period to get your feet under you, get familiar with the business, and know where you really need to take it. That said—again, should you get the job—you have my full permission to make any changes that you'd like."

I knew then that I'd gotten the job. I was hired into a company that eventually brought me face-to-face with a prolonged investigation and court case (detailed earlier in chapter 2). Having such high-level support made all the difference when it came time to make hard decisions for the good of the company. My experience in that business and the colleagues I served with is ranked now as a highlight in my career.

CORE UNDERLYING BELIEFS

Had I not allowed my ambition and curiosity to be stronger than my doubts and fears, I never would have considered applying for that position. Getting the job was a victory, to be sure. Yet as I mentioned previously, my own concerns about being young and inexperienced limited me for a time in that role.

This has been a recurring theme for me throughout my career: going up for new roles that stretch me in new ways, getting pay raises, and climbing the corporate ladder with ambition and drive. Yet each time, I'm met with the worrying thought that this will be the time when I slip completely out of my depth and drown.

My wife has asked me, "When are you going to feel good enough?"

Unfortunately, I'm not entirely sure that I will. As far as I can tell, some negative beliefs and stress never truly go away. For those that fall into this category, we have to learn how to respond well to them. Sometimes, rightly or wrongly, we mask them. Some masks cover our sadness with a smile and a happy face. Others portray confidence when we're shaking in our boots.

From the facades we all create, it is an easy leap of logic to then wonder what people would think of us if they really knew who we were and what we were thinking. We grow attached to the image that we project, rather than our authentic selves. And many also struggle with weak humility where their beliefs create imbalance in the duality of being both nothing and everything. Some hold to the belief mentioned earlier that they are the sum of the whole versus an essential part.

Feeling like you are the sum of the whole of humanity, I have learned, does not necessarily mean that you think you are better than everyone else. It often means that you think you have to go it alone. You detach yourself from others and make your strength the only strength available to you. Now you are the sum of the whole. You cut ties from others who can help. This leaves us feeling obligated to be all strength and no weakness and it gives no room for error. It creates overwhelm and constant strain. Heavy loads get heavier and the chances for reprieve get removed. It means that people need to see us in a certain light but inside, since this is all founded on incorrect beliefs, we struggle—and thus, imposter syndrome is born.

By definition, imposter syndrome is a limiting belief about ourselves. It tells us that we are inadequate or incompetent, or a failure in some way—often in spite of evidence to the contrary. We can see areas where we have been skilled or successful, but our feelings about ourselves don't match up with reality. A nicer way of looking at it might be that we believe we're something that we're not, when the evidence proves we are something better.

On that basis, I suppose we are nearly all imposters—we are all much better than we think we are.

Dr. Valerie Young, author of *The Secret Thoughts of Successful Women* did the work of categorizing imposter syndrome into five subgroups, each carrying their own set of negative beliefs. These categories are: the perfectionist, the superhero, the natural genius, the soloist, and the expert.[21]

The perfectionist sets excessively high goals for themselves, then experiences major self-doubt when they don't think they can measure up. They can be control freaks, believing that something done right has to be done themselves.

I relate the most to this variation, aligning myself with the limiting beliefs of perfectionism and all-or-nothing thinking. I might decide that effective weight loss requires going to the gym at least three times a week, running in between, utilizing intermittent fasting to stop eating after six at night, and following a completely different diet than what I have now. While

---

21 Valerie Young, *The Secret Thoughts of Successful Women*, Currency, 2011. As featured by Melody Wilding, "The Five Types Of Impostor Syndrome And How To Beat Them," *Fast Company*. Accessed Online, January 2020. https://www.fastcompany.com/40421352/the-five-types-of-impostor-syndrome-and-how-to-beat-them.

that might be a justifiably high standard for life, it's also true that I will never be able to make all of those changes at once. So what will I do? Nothing at all.

The superhero imposter is trickier to spot from the outside. Their negative belief is more internal, believing they are the only phony amongst everyone else who is the real deal. Workaholic tendencies serve as a cover-up for their own insecurities. They push themselves to work harder and harder in order to measure up to everyone else, which creates a name for themselves. They hear things like, "You're such a hard worker!" and "You're always the last one in the office, aren't you great?" and "You stayed up so late to get that project done, good on you."

If perfectionism is fed by impatience, then the superhero is driven by a need for approval. Ultimately, they believe they have to work harder than everyone else around them just to prove their worth. The intensity of the need for approval is excessive for the superhero, in that everyone has to validate them in order for them to acknowledge their place in the world. They panic when someone is upset because, in their mind, they are of no value if that person doesn't think so.

That means the superhero isn't always the one working the hardest but is sometimes the one running around doing good for everyone to the exclusion of their own needs. We praise them for being kind and compassionate and sacrificial. And that is the praise that encourages them to keep going, because without that external validation, they have nothing.

At times, it's a strength to be able to learn quickly—but that isn't enough for the natural genius imposter, who judges their competence on ease and speed as opposed to effort. If it takes a long time to master something, they feel ashamed and useless. They have to be the one to get there the fastest, and they tie their self-worth up in that speed.

The natural genius expects to be able to pick something up on the first try rather than giving themselves time to learn. I often see this expressed in the behavior of some of my younger children (though this is not age-related!). If they can't be great at tennis right away, for example, they don't want to play. This expands out into their limiting beliefs with "should" statements. I should be able to do this now...Life should be more fair...This shouldn't happen to me...That person shouldn't be suffering... This should happen faster...This shouldn't be that hard...

The danger here is in creating rules for the world that don't actually exist.

The soloist is closely related to the natural genius in their beliefs, convinced that they can never ask for help. For this imposter, interconnectivity reveals their inadequacies. It isn't that they don't want help, but that they believe they only demonstrate their worth by doing everything themselves. This imposter is driven by negative self-labeling; they tell themselves that they are irretrievably flawed or unlikeable and that those flaws must remain hidden if they want to be liked.

Last but not least, the expert imposter measures their confidence and worth based on how much they know and can do, all while believing none of it will ever be enough. They are constantly trying to prove their competence in an unprovable way.

This imposter is driven by the fear of being exposed as inexperienced or unknowledgeable, which keeps them from pursuing new experiences and opportunities. Their negative belief is to discount the positives, including their accomplishments and successes, only seeing their shortcomings and failures.

OTHER LIMITING SELF-BELIEFS

What we do is the fruit of what we think, feel, and believe. If we truly want to change our behavior, become empowered, and be the best possible version of ourselves, then we have to begin with our thoughts. Other limiting beliefs include:

- Catastrophizing: A disaster is around the corner and everything is about to collapse. Coupled with an excessive need for approval, this can be layered onto the belief that *everything is all my fault*.
- Mindreading: We can tell people don't like us based on the way that they behave, regardless of what they say.
- Disqualifying the present: We'll be able to relax later after we get one more thing done. Yet if we never allow time to rest, always rushing into the future, our best possible state is panicked and jittery, which makes it difficult or impossible to become patient with our circumstances.
- Dwelling on the past: If we could only figure it out, then we wouldn't repeat it. We convince ourselves that we can analyze our pain excessively, beating ourselves up because of what went wrong in the past.
- Pessimism: Life is meant to be garbage, without any meaning or happiness. It's turning to face the adversity and then deciding it's not worth fighting. That's just the way it is. Life sucks, so deal with it.

If we're not careful, we can convince ourselves that these beliefs are assets. Perfectionism masks as high standards. Disqualifying the present masks as ambition. Low self-worth masks as humility.[22] Yet we're held back from an empowered sense of self when we only hold these me-centric beliefs, isolating us and turning our focus inward.

Instead of battling individual beliefs, we need to get to the bottom of why we're wearing a mask at all. Knowing who we truly are and what we're capable of rightly places our self-worth on the purpose we're meant to pursue, our relationships to others around us, and the value of our part in this miraculous world. It's knowing that we are loved and of value, without a need to prove it to anyone.

True humility is recognizing that there is power in the collective to change the world, and that our part to play in it matters. It is a belief so empowering that it can get us out of our seats to actually do something of significance in the world.

SEALED WITH GRATITUDE

The word *grateful,* by way of etymology, came into the English language around the 1500s, from the Latin *gratus* meaning pleasing. Previously, we focused on appreciation more than gratitude, because great suffering is not always pleasing but is almost always of value. Here, however, I want us to return our focus to gratitude.

If your bank only gave you an account of your balance when you were in overdraft, you wouldn't stay with that bank for long. Instead, they tell us everything—the good and the bad—and give us credit where credit is due.

---

22 John Kotter wrote a fantastic book called *A Sense of Urgency* that further explores counterfeit emotions.

When you do take an account of your life, then make sure to measure the good as well. Take time to feel gratitude for what's pleasing, as well as to appreciate what's not.

The Victorian-era artist James McNeill Whistler once painted a tiny picture of roses that he loved so much he kept it to himself. His followers were frustrated by that because they loved it too and wanted to add it to their collections. Whistler refused time and again. When asked why he wouldn't sell it, one of his most excellent works, he said this:

> "Whenever I feel that my hand has lost its cunning, whenever I doubt my ability, I look at that little picture of the spray of roses and say to myself, 'Whistler, you painted that. Your hand drew it. Your imagination conceived the colors, your skill put the roses on the canvas.' And I know that what I have done I can do again."[23]

Then he continued with wisdom we all can follow: "Hang on the walls of your mind the memory of your successes. Take counsel from your strength, not your weakness. Think of the good jobs you've done."

It's easy to be grateful when something big and exciting happens. If you were to win the lottery, you'd be immediately grateful. Promotions and pay raises are filled with gratitude as well. But let's look beyond the obvious and be more grateful. Even the smaller things, like having breakfast this morning, enjoying another day to live and breathe and move, the smile from a stranger as they pass by. All of these things can add up when we count them and lead to a very full account of reasons to be happy.

---

23 As told by American author and religious leader Sterling W. Sill.

Sadly, too many of us don't give ourselves credit for the good things we've accomplished. A grateful disposition certainly doesn't remove our challenges, but it can give us improved perspective and added strength to respond well.

If I'm grateful for the opportunities that I've been given, then I'll make the most of them. If I'm grateful for the people around me, I'll love and serve them more. If I'm grateful for the skills I've been given, I'll hone them and expand on them.

If I have a role to play, I'm going to play it well, which will enrich the whole, and I'll continue to nurture this ever-expanding circle of potential power to do good, become more, and thrive. It shifts our perspective away from the symptomatology of suffering into the greater plane of purpose and meaning. And when suffering and joy carry purpose, we find even greater individual and collective power.

A FINAL WORD ON APPRECIATING THE STRUGGLE

Before we walk through each of the seven virtues in Part II, understand that they are not my aspirations or lightly held beliefs. These are deeply rooted beliefs, actions, and character components, time-tested and honored. Without them, our potential loss is the loss of our potential. As they say, you can count the seeds in an apple, but you can't count the number of apples in a seed.

As a word of caution, however, there is a significant cost in refusing to nurture these virtues in the face of adversity. By refusing to face our struggles—to break open and begin to grow as a seed, or to dissolve and reform as a butterfly—our relationships are at risk. We cannot nurture connection if we are buried under perpetual stress. We cannot find our purpose in life if we aren't willing to follow the direction life is leading us.

There is a cost taken out of our self-esteem, quality of life, relationships, and ability to make a difference in the world.

Refusing to grow is an option, but it's a selfish one. You can't build a business or live a life that only serves yourself personally and then expect it to be strong and enduring. This is bigger than you and me. We're simply playing small but valuable parts in a big, wide world. This is the nature of humility. It demands boldness, courage, and conviction.

In the first section of this book, we explored the necessity of adversity and its essential relationship to life's purpose and meaning. We have a responsibility to humbly accept it when it comes. Not in a sense of defeat, but in a conscious acceptance of it so we can courageously confront it, understand it, and be changed by it. The next step in this process, therefore, is the acquisition of our seven vital virtues, with the first being the development of a disciplined heart.

Why are we developing these virtues? Because we are choosing to not be shackled to suffering or to wallow in the mire of self-pity but to choose bravely and enthusiastically to be the masters of our own destiny. Adversity often happens *to* us, even if it is because of us. Choosing to develop these virtues puts us back in the driver's seat of our own life. It is the cultivation of joy amidst adversity rather than succumbing to whatever might spring up.

TAKE STOCK OF SELF-WORTH
AND CONNECTION

The chapters to come ask us to face challenging tasks and difficult truths. As you pursue the challenges of personal growth in the face of struggle, take stock when happiness, fulfillment, and strength follow as a consequence of that effort. It will be by degrees, but when do the first few degrees appear?

- From what we have discussed in the previous chapter, how would you define humility?
- How does understanding we are both everything and nothing inform our choices when we struggle?
- If reaching out for support in your particular set of challenges is daunting, what can help you make the right choice?
- What are some essential benefits that flow into our lives as we develop greater humility?

Part II

THE SEVEN VIRTUES: THE ELEMENTS OF GROWTH TOWARD EMPOWERMENT

How happy is he born and taught
That serveth not another's will;
Whose armour is his honest thought,
And simple truth his utmost skill!

Whose passions not his masters are;
Whose soul is still prepared for death,
Untied unto the world by care
Of public fame or private breath;

Who envies none that chance doth raise,
Nor vice; who never understood
How deepest wounds are given by praise;
Nor rules of state, but rules of good;

Who hath his life from rumours freed;
Whose conscience is his strong retreat;
Whose state can neither flatterers feed,
Nor ruin make oppressors great;

Who God doth late and early pray
More of His grace than gifts to lend;
And entertains the harmless day
With a religious book or friend;

—This man is freed from servile bands
Of hope to rise or fear to fall:
Lord of himself, though not of lands,
And having nothing, yet hath all.

—SIR HENRY WOTTON,
"THE CHARACTER OF A HAPPY LIFE"

Chapter 4

VIRTUE #1: A DISCIPLINED HEART

STRONG CHARACTER IS BORN OF NOBLE ACTION, WHICH IS CONCEIVED FIRST OF NOBLE DESIRE

A number of years ago in Birmingham, England, I hosted a training meeting for an audience of small business owners. One of our topics was the need to establish meaningful goals that would take them from where they were to where they needed to be. At the heart of that discussion was the principle that a compelling *why* will create a meaningful *how*. A strong sense of purpose facilitates every action and result that follows.

As we worked through the exercise together, the business owners in the room answered questions like, "What do you want to achieve?" "Why are you here?" and "What brings you to this space?" We heard all sorts of stories, including one woman who spoke with fire in her eyes about her health and well-being business. She used words like *passionate* and *overwhelming* and *gift* as she described her goal of giving people their vitality back.

When I asked her where she found all of the emotion that had clearly driven her toward a clear and ambitious purpose, she began to tear up. She told us about the terminal illness she had battled and how she spent years facing an unknown future. Now that she was in remission, she wanted to share the gift of a healthy life with her clients. It was truly inspiring, not only for her and her business, but for everyone in the room.

Behind her, another woman raised her hand. Her eyes were fiery as well, but with frustration. She boldly said, "I've got a concern with that."

I gave her the floor, and she continued, "I've never overcome a terminal illness. I'm not saying I want one. But her great 'why' came from great suffering, and that's not something I can access. I have a vision, but I don't have that kind of experience to anchor it in. What do I do with that? I feel like a big tree with little roots."

Before answering her myself, I checked in with the rest of the group. I asked whether others felt inspired but somewhat frustrated by these stories of great hardship—who else was feeling like a big tree with little roots?

About 80 percent of the room raised their hands. Most people felt connected to a life purpose in some way but also felt the connection was superficial or too weak.

What frustrates many people who feel like big trees with little roots is that they overlook the time required for the roots to grow and balance the tree's top. If the big tree represents our vision for our future life, then the roots represent our desires to achieve it. Desire takes time to grow and most certainly requires nurturing and our keenest attention. The tree and the root system in this metaphor don't grow at equal paces. Vision can be captured in a moment or developed in a short period of time, but the strong desires required to realize it and enjoy its fruits demand much more of us.

The essential *why* to our *how* is the disciplined heart to the educated mind. There are many life or business gurus out there that promote instantaneous change through the discovery of their secrets and life messages, but the fact is, our minds may be enlightened in a moment, but our hearts take time to change and it requires meaningful transformation for lasting behavioral change to stick. So, I am the bearer of bad news here: this step requires your devoted commitment over time. But its benefits last longer than the fleeting feeling that the sudden surge of enlightenment can offer.

> Our minds may be enlightened in a moment, but our hearts take time to change and it requires meaningful transformation for lasting behavioral change to stick.

WE NEED MORE THAN PASSION

We are often told to follow our passions, especially when crafting a *why* that can justify great ambition. Often, we're directed to choose something we already feel inclined to pursue. Natural talents and interests or knowledge and interest that comes from a deeply personal struggle create a sense of passion that's easy to follow.

Thinking back to elementary school subjects, someone who isn't "good at math" will not likely join the math club, but a natural inclination toward athletics or the arts makes hours of after-school pursuits fly by.

For example, two of my favorite subjects in high school were art and music. If I wasn't in the music department during breaks, I could be found painting in the art department. When it came to music, I picked up my instrument very quickly and did well with it. My music teacher was excellent, and the constant reassurance from him and rapport with us as students made it easy to keep playing, learning, and growing in skill.

Near the end of portfolio deadlines one year, my music teacher noticed that I wasn't in his department as much, and asked if he could come look at my artwork in the neighboring department. As one might expect, I was chuffed—absolutely beaming with pride. With so much positive reinforcement from him in my music classes, and now an interest in my development in other subjects, I looked forward to what he might have to say about this other budding talent of mine.

On lunch break, he found me working in the art room on one of my projects. He went over to speak with my art teacher and to look at some of my previous work. I listened in, hopeful I would overhear more reinforcement of natural abilities. As my music teacher looked through my artwork, the feedback from my art teacher was not quite what I'd hoped: "I'm not an artist," said my music teacher, "so help me understand. Is Ben's work any good? How does he compare to the other kids?"

Leaning closer to hear what was sure to be a validating response, my heart sank as my art teacher replied, "You know, Ben's not the best artist in the class."

I admit, I was mildly disappointed. Having what I felt was a natural gift had motivated me so much in music class, and I was sure that was why art was so enjoyable as well.

My art teacher continued with a lesson I've never forgotten. "He does do better than most, though. Not because he's more talented, but because he works harder."

A degree of talent can only get us so far, but hard work takes us down new roads. With hard work, I improved my skill and performance in art, which fed my passion there in ways that passion fed my hard work in music. To summarize: hard work feeds passion, and passion feeds hard work. Both are required, which is why this virtue isn't simply to "have heart," but to have a disciplined one.

Fantastically, the relationship of passion and hard work is rooted in etymology. So you don't need to simply take my word for it. The word "passion" dates back to a reference to the physical suffering of Christ. Its root comes from the past participle stem of the Latin word *pati*, meaning to endure, undergo, or experience. With its connection to the divine, the word expanded to include the suffering of martyrs, and then suffering in general. From these same roots, we gained the word compassion, which means to suffer with someone. It wasn't until the late fourteenth century that the word began to mean strong emotion or desire.

Perhaps there still remains some divinity in our suffering, given the power for revolutionary change that can attend it. Great struggle is the schoolmaster that can transform mediocrity into mastery and mastery into meaning if we allow disciplined hearts the chance to temper our passions.

But let's not misunderstand the role of passion. Author and

speaker, Terri Trespicio wisely taught that finding our passion suggests that we've lost it. She also suggests that most people approach the subject not just badly, but annoyingly! On an article on her website, she says this:

> "You know what everyone tells me their passion is? Helping people. Yawn. That's not a passion; that's a prosocial instinct that we're born with to keep us from (completely) annihilating each other and isolating ourselves. It makes you human and not a monster. Saying your passion is helping people is no different than saying you're busy. Everyone is. And to say either thing as a way of distinguishing yourself is to assume the other person isn't, and it just never lands right. (I'm busy AND passionate, too, thank you very much!)"[24]

Let's not confuse the unique passion we need to direct our lives and fuel our purpose with basic, natural human emotions everyone else experiences. How banal. Perhaps, like the martyrs of the past, our true passion and life's mission may be found in the seat of our personal suffering. And like many people of today, it can also be found in what we truly love and value. Either way, passion requires tempering, discipline, and commitment to mature and be truly fruitful.

PRECEDED BY DESIRE

Desire, by definition, is a wish—to want, crave, or covet something. In practice, it is a wish that we long for. The significance of the word is in its strength. It is a craving so strong that we are sent off in that direction. Consequently, whatever we desire becomes the direction in which we are aimed—it determines

---

24 Terri Trespicio, "Stop Searching for Your Passion (Do This Instead)," TerriTrespicio.com. Accessed Online January, 2020. https://territrespicio.com/passion/.

what we achieve and who we become. Lamentably, this is true even if we do not understand our desires or their consequences.

Over time, even our most private desires will be revealed by the actions we take. We become what we repeatedly think about whether we like it or not.

Certainly, there are external factors such as genetics, biology, circumstances, and environment that affect our lot in life. However, there is a domain within all of us ruled by personal responsibility, and that is the jurisdiction of desire. To realize the vision for who we become and the life we hope to create, we must take responsibility for the desires that we cultivate into action, from the smallest wish to the deepest intention.

From a foundational starting point, the human conscience itself can be considered a desire connected to personal responsibility.

With a few pathological exceptions, everyone has an innate, almost universal standard of right and wrong. It is at least a flicker of direction, if not a great flame that inherently limits and directs our actions. We grow from our first interactions as toddlers to more mature interpersonal relationships in adulthood by recognizing the gift of our own conscience and responding to it. It becomes more than a signal of right or wrong, but a form of internal accountability that helps us to be self-directed in our own development. Our responsibility is to give heat to the flame, training our desires and actions to become more virtuous as we mature.

THE CYCLES OF ACTION AND EMOTION

If you're a person who feels like a big tree with shallow roots, that your ambition outpaces your purpose, look closely at your day-to-day actions. I've heard it said, "Tell me what you think about when you don't have to think, and I'll tell you what kind of person you are." If you want to understand what your real desires are, look at the ways you spend your time.

The tree might not be as big as you once thought. For as much as we say that we're motivated to achieve great things, without the consistency of action, we cannot grow our ambition or our roots. Likewise, the pursuit of personal change—growing from who we are to who we want to be—requires the training of our desires to align with the path we want to take. It is a discipline focused on the heart.

Training events for personal development can often include a "find your why" or vision-framing experience because the strength of your actions is set by the strength of your emotions. In a literal, scientific sense, when we act out of what we're truly feeling, change happens faster. The neural pathways in the brain that lead to emotional centers are shorter than those that lead to the cognitive centers. Consequently, we feel faster than we think.

We can only read so many books, listen to so many speakers, or attempt so many formulas before falling back on desires that are triggered by strong emotion. The task we have in our self-directed learning is to align what we know cognitively with what we feel, and then demonstrate sufficient mastery of our emotions to ensure appropriate harmony between the two.

This is the true nature of the *why* we are so often asked to identify: a focused desire that is strong enough to counter all competing inclinations along the way.

Wonderfully, the paradox of desire allows us to temper emotion with action as much as we fuel action by emotion. Like Newton's Second Law, each act of tempered desire, however small, adds to our momentum of personal growth. As action follows feeling, feeling follows action. Noble desire gives birth to noble action, which matures over time to give us a strong character, reflected through maturing emotional responses. Therefore, we lead with disciplined desires and their related actions to see success, allow passion to ensue, and inspire true change to take root.

> If thought is father to the deed, emotion is mother to the thought.

STANDING AGAINST THE WIND

Deprivation can teach us a great deal about our true desires. Shortly after I was married, my wife and I developed food poisoning. In a bittersweet but oddly romantic sense, we had never felt so sick in our lives, but at least we were together for it. Once the illness lifted a bit, I remember feeling incredible, like food had never tasted as good before then.

Similarly, my dad was literally on the other side of the world for almost all of my childhood, living in Wales while I lived in New Zealand. I didn't see him a single time from the age of fourteen to twenty-two. He'd send an occasional letter with a promise to visit, followed by an excuse for why he hadn't come already. Each time he broke my heart, I thought, "When I'm a dad, I'm going to be as hands-on as I can be." Such deprivations of health and a present father in these two examples served to increase my appreciation and desire for well-being and fueled my desires to be a great dad when the opportunity presented itself.

Not all deprivation is externally forced, however. With discipline, we will, by necessity, eliminate some actions and behaviors from our lives, and that is when our true desires will make themselves known. C.S. Lewis explains this struggle as follows:

"No man knows how bad he is until he has tried very hard to be good. A silly idea is current, that good people do not know what temptation means. This is an obvious lie. Only those who try to resist temptation know how strong it is. After all, you find out the strength of the German army by fighting against it, not by giving in. You find out the strength of a wind by trying to walk against it, not by lying down. A man who gives in to temptation after five minutes simply does not know what it would have been like an hour later…Bad people, in one sense, know very little about badness. They've lived a sheltered life by always giving in. We never find out the strength of the evil impulse inside us until we try to fight it."[25]

In the early days of a friend of mine recovering from alcoholism, his wife confided in me, "Sometimes I find that when he is sober, I prefer him as a drunk. Without alcohol as his coping mechanism, he is irritable, angry, impetuous, and difficult to live with." From the outside looking in, my friend had the appearance of a better person before he was sober—but this was only the façade of placated, unchecked desire. The strength of that hold on his life was only made known by his willingness to resist it.

The sacrifice of desires reveals our true nature, for better or worse, made clear by our refusal to give in.

---

25   C.S. Lewis, *Mere Christianity*, Geoffrey Bles, 1952.

The stage of discipline that requires us to stand up against the wind or to face the army is a difficult one. Taming our desires reveals just how strong they are, and it requires time, patience, practice, and selflessness to overcome.

FOR THINGS TO CHANGE, FIRST I MUST CHANGE

We have all realized, by this stage of life, that intrinsic motivation is unreliable. I am not absolved of my responsibility simply because I lack the energy to remain disciplined. Thus, the search for incentives begins. What can we do to keep ourselves, our employees, our organizations, and our families consistently moving toward a desired goal?

In a commercial environment, for example, one might think that we share a core financial desire, especially for entrepreneurs and high performers, but research done by Dr. Kathleen Vohs at the University of Minnesota says otherwise. When prodded with financial incentives, the participants in her study showed, amongst other things, a significantly *reduced* willingness to volunteer assistance to a stranger and a significantly *greater* physical separation when seated across from a person during an introductory conversation.

The true drivers for the entrepreneurs that she studied were far, far different:

- The thrill of competition.
- The desire for adventure.
- The joy of creation.
- The satisfaction of team building.
- The desire to achieve meaning in life.

The opportunity to fulfill any one of these desires motivated them to take risks in pursuit of their goals in ways that money could not inspire.[26]

For the entrepreneur, CEO, and high-performing leader, each of these factors works together, shaping the need to transform themselves in order to protect their business. Mahatma Gandhi famously taught that we must be the change we wish to see—that for things to change, first I must change. This is true for any person, movement, or organization. It takes individual transformation to reshape the whole, often starting from the most visible players. All eyes are on them as the chief role models before anything else.

To increase an organization's performance, the most successful CEO leads by example in both operational excellence and from a framework of social harmony. Matthew Lieberman, a professor of psychology at UCLA, defined the challenge of this pursuit in an article in *Harvard Business Review*.[27] He pointed to research that indicated the discord of a simultaneous relational focus and process focus. In fact, the two come from different parts of the brain that do not work at the same time. Neural imaging studies show that the two networks function like a seesaw—as one engages, the other grows quiet.

In other words, we literally fight against the processes of the brain to get the best outcomes. Evidence supports this struggle and the rewards that the successful are given. Dave Carvajal,

---

26   "What Drives the Best Entrepreneurs? Hint: It's Not Money," *Forbes*, February 2013. https://www.forbes.com/sites/groupthink/2013/02/13/what-drives-the-best-entrepreneurs-hint-its-not-money/#2a73ed964348.

27   Matthew Lieberman, "Should Leaders Focus on Results, or on People?," *Harvard Business Review*, December 2013. https://hbr.org/2013/12/should-leaders-focus-on-results-or-on-people.

CEO of Dave Partners, an Executive Search and Leadership Development firm, notes that those who combine these skills and effectively shift between the two parts of their brain are rated as "great leaders" 72 percent of the time.[28]

As a former president of a sizable international business and as a husband and father, I've found that the need for operational excellence and social harmony, combined with personal example, are not criteria reserved for those within a corporate environment. Arguably, we all share their imperative. What are we, if not the chief executive officers of our own lives? Do we not have the responsibility to take reasonable risk to captain our own destinies? Do our children not follow our example more than our verbal instruction? Wouldn't you agree that our personal lives crave more balance between order and harmony? These disciplines are prerequisites for a good life.

In our attempts to start with a strong *why*, we often miss this need for a strong character. The combination of the two ensures clarity in the vision and strength in our response to it. How often have we watched as people in our lives who lack character continually make bad choices? They misinterpret relationships, compromise circumstances, and miss opportunities because they don't see things as they really are, and they fail to act with wisdom.

To be empowered with both vision and character, something within us has to connect with a clear and inspiring future state, in spite of the challenges.

---

28   Dave Carvajal, "The Strongest Desire of Every CEO," *AlleyWatch*, April 2017. https://www.alleywatch.com/2017/04/strongest-desire-every-ceo/.

CULTIVATED, WEEDED, AND NURTURED

I used to want to press everything as hard as it could go. I'd sprint along every chance that I could, trying to reach a new and ambitious vision, and often I would run out of steam. Then I'd change my plans and sprint in another direction, only to burn out yet again. Early on in my marriage, I noticed that my wife didn't share that pattern. I described the difference to her, a little bit frustrated that we weren't on the same track.

I explained that it was as if we were walking up the same mountain together, striving to climb it as husband and wife, but we weren't taking the same path or keeping the same pace. My path up the mountain was a bit like the flight of a bumblebee, darting around and racing ahead, then falling backward when I need to rest. I would get lost in the trees and lose the path, then come back to it for a moment only to lose it again. Every now and then, our paths would cross, and she would still be marching forward, persistently walking the same path at the same pace.

She thought for a moment, agreed, and then asked me, "Which way do you think is better?"

"I *know* which way is better," I answered. "I just wish that I could do it."

Fortunately, while a leopard can't change its spots, human beings change all the time! In the years since that realization, I've slowly been able to train my desires to a set path. I might lose that path now and then, but I can find it again and move forward with purpose, following disciplined desires toward my ultimate goals.

Now, rather than a busy bumblebee darting all over the place, I envision a gardener who spends deliberate and much enjoyed time tending plants around their home. Being in the soil is refreshing to them—the smell and the feel of it reminds them of spring and excites them for all the new life to come. They spend time each day carefully tending to those plants, paying close attention to the needs of each. They train unruly vines to stakes and trellises to bring them into discipline and order so that they might bear more fruit. They feed the soil, pull out the weeds, clip back overgrowth, and bring a few extra flowers in for the vase on their windowsill.

The strongest roots grow in proportion to our experience and in accordance with what we can manage, not by manufacturing stress over what we cannot control. As the garden would not exist without the gardener's careful touch, so must we begin our journey toward discipline with intention. Nothing truly begins until someone wills it so.

The experience is not to be hurried, forcing our will into a new shape all at once. By giving the journey the patience that it requires, inspired by connection to others around us, and in acceptance and gratitude of the circumstances we've been given, discipline becomes something much more attainable—even enjoyable. Even if our vision is small, or we change our mind and come back to it later, if we can recognize and appreciate the value of the journey, then we can pace ourselves accordingly. Don't beat yourself up if this process of growth takes a little time. You're in good company.

THE DISCIPLINE OF PATIENCE

Sometimes seasons have to pass before we bear the fruit of our desires. Patience in that season is not simply waiting for a passage of time to expire, which will happen regardless of what we do. It is to let time pass well, remaining steadfast as it does.

As the saying goes, "In patience, possess ye your souls." The inverse is true as well: in impatience, we lose them. Without nurturing a root system of character to spread out deep and wide within the soil where we've been planted, the weight of the tree becomes too much to bear, and we often give up.

Sometimes it feels like we cannot change our desires until we have an overwhelming desire to do so. That is wonderfully and frustratingly ironic, isn't it? But even those who have the experience of trauma or great suffering to inspire their vision must constantly train their desires in order to maintain them.

The practice of changing our character—which includes disciplining our desires and our hearts—is a journey, not an event. The ability to endure our struggles will always demand a degree of patience. The realization of our hopes and dreams demands it too.

THE SUPPORTING STRENGTH OF HUMILITY

Because desires are emotion-driven, they are often quite inwardly focused. Displays of selfishness are signals of untrained desire.

The limiting beliefs we covered in chapter 3 all had one thing in common: they were all focused on self. As much as we need to get outside ourselves to develop humility, we need that same perspective to surrender to challenge, train our desires, and develop our character. Happiness and fulfillment demands this letting go of private will and self-interest. It requires some surrender and sacrifice of some things now, both good and bad, in order to achieve the very best things later.

Without humility, adversity will challenge my patience with the process. I cannot accept the struggle if I believe I'm above it in some way. Humility gives strength to our purpose, a reason for being that expands our capacity for patience along the way.

As we do good, we start to feel good, and when we feel good, we want to do more of what caused it. We start to see that there is much more than the discomfort of discipline. Stepping out of our self-centered perspective, then, is a way to push momentum forward. The longer we stand against the wind, the more experience we gain, and the more confidence we have to reinforce the desires we hope to train.

THE DISCIPLINE OF ACCEPTANCE AND GRATITUDE

One of two things will spark the cultivation and discipline of our desires: suffering or service. Either I will suffer so deeply that I will experience humility and a desire to change out of necessity, or I will reach out beyond myself, serve others, and become humbled and uplifted by our interconnectivity. Either works and sometimes they happen together.

Gratitude for the circumstances we've been given and the strength and support we have to learn from them is the wellspring of all other virtues. It creates personal refinement in ways that nothing else can.

Changing our character is a journey, not an event.

Take time to express gratitude for the air you breathe, the sun that shines, the health you have, the loved ones in your life, the country you live in. Express gratitude for the trials and adversity that you experience—and if not gratitude, then appreciation. Express it inwardly, to be reflected in your choices. Express it to others, lifting you both up with kindness and connection.

Weave gratitude into your life and over time, it will open your eyes up to opportunities, strength, determination, a disciplined heart, and a passionate desire.

Like the seasons of the year, there are cyclical patterns in our lives that continually feed into each other. The more we experience, the more we find meaning. The clearer this meaning becomes, the more it gives us patience. The more humility we patiently express, the more we can be strengthened by our experiences. The vicious cycle of repeated suffering transforms into a virtuous cycle of growth and prosperity.

MEASURED WINS ALONG THE WAY

I'm reassured that who I am today is not who I was a few years ago. And as I look at my present self with honesty, I'm so grateful that who I am today will not reflect who I can become in the future. Our capacity for personal transformation is beyond incredible. (Thank goodness!)

While it is important to track progress toward our destinations, we often measure the results of our efforts to the exclusion of the efforts themselves. Yes, we of course want visible change and progress, but sometimes when change is slow coming and habit requires repeated efforts to pick ourselves up again and again, it helps to measure our efforts too.

Every right choice is worth celebrating.

There have been times in my life where deeply entrenched bad habits have knocked me down. New to the commitment to improve, I'd pick myself up with enthusiasm and try again. But over the course of many years, a couple of habits simply didn't go away like I wanted them to. I found myself slowly getting discouraged at my failure to eliminate them. I fell into a trap of measuring perfection versus improvement and then in measuring only behavior without considering the improvement of my heart.

As I started to measure my progress differently, I saw that while I hadn't perfectly eliminated certain habits, I had improved them. Additionally, the repeated efforts had developed new qualities that grounded me and acquainted me well with commitment, persistence, devotion, empathy, understanding, tolerance, acceptance, forgiveness, and so on.

We admire character in others, often forgetting that it's developed over time and with struggle and discipline. It comes with a high price tag: the expense of what we want in the moment. But strong though they may be, our desires are not in control of us. We choose to give in or to train them in a better direction.

As you look for evidence of this discipline in your life, go easy on yourself. Don't beat yourself up. This isn't permission to make excuses and rationalize poor conduct, but to ensure we get a balanced perspective that a disciplined heart requires more of us than we originally realize. That's okay. Give yourself manageable steps that you can follow toward the ultimate outcome. Celebrate the pursuit of your vision, and notice when your character has begun to develop. Because it's not just about the behavior, but about who we're becoming in the process.

WANTING TO START

If change feels overwhelming or impossible and you simply can't believe it will happen, rest assured that such belief is not the starting point. The starting point is to want to believe.

By cultivating your desire to believe, you can begin to make and measure small steps toward the mark. Evidence of progress will give you confidence that you can do it and bigger steps become possible. With patience and humility, you will not only achieve your goal, but become more than you realized as a result.

- How does your vision for the future compare with your commitment to it?
- What desires get in the way of your progress?
- Name some steps you are taking now, or will take, to train your desires to align with your vision.
- What role does patience play in the need to train your heart?
- Why does humility feature in this chapter? What does it have to do with patience and discipline?

Chapter 5

VIRTUE #2: AN EDUCATED MIND

AS A DISCIPLINED HEART FOCUSES THE MIND, SO AN EDUCATED MIND TRAINS THE HEART

I received my degree later in life than many. At the age of twenty-three, I moved back to the United Kingdom with the hope of getting to know my father as I hadn't seen him since I was fourteen years old. I had worked for a small ad agency in Auckland, New Zealand prior to that point, and now I thought I would seize the opportunity to pursue my degree and expand my graphic design opportunities.

Once enrolled, I fell head over heels, almost from day one. Having some industry experience already, classroom results were easy to come by. And as successes tend to do, the rewards of good work grew my passion by leaps and bounds. Not only was I happy with my performance, but I began to envision a future beyond the degree—how I could utilize my education to become an art director or designer long-term. I was in my element, through and through.

But it was not to last.

On my way into school, about halfway through the first semester, my tutor stopped me. He apologized before he began, then explained that there had been a problem with my application.

I had been born in the UK, my parents were British, and I had a passport, citizenship, and family all living there. But I was reared in New Zealand and had lived in Australia for a couple of years before coming back. As my tutor explained to me, my residence didn't count until I had lived in the country for at least three consecutive years before enrolling. Consequently, I was labeled an overseas student, and I was not entitled to any student loans, grants, or financial support because of it. If I wanted to continue my studies, I had to pay my fees up-front, right then, equivalent to the annual income I collected from my part-time job.

I looked around him to the stairs that led to the class I was meant to take. Without a commitment to pay, he couldn't let me go to class.

I fought back tears as I turned to go back to my car, which I had regrettably purchased on finance (for the first and last time in my life). I collected my things and drove back to my home, not sure what I was going to do next.

My mum and the family I grew up with, who I really needed in that moment, were on the other side of the world. I had no chance to further my income and no chance to further my education. I felt trapped. In that same month, my stepsister passed away in New Zealand, and I had no resources to travel to her funeral, which I desperately wanted to attend. My girlfriend, who was my closest friend, dumped me, and my father was charged with crimes that would put him in prison for a long time.

That was it. I had absolutely nothing left. It was me and a part-time job, alone on the other side of the world from everything and almost everyone I knew and loved.

But as the saying goes, "weeping may endure for a moment but joy cometh in the morning." Slowly that horrible season of life started to shift from a bitter winter to a magnificent spring. My girlfriend, thankfully, changed her mind. About a year and a half later, Kim and I were married.

Over the years, my career blossomed and my family thrived, but I felt increasingly frustrated that I didn't have my degree. My connection to formal studies had been taken from me, but that did not remove my responsibility to continue to gain knowledge throughout my life. The goal had been left undone for too long and—as a sales director for seventeen markets, established in my career, with five children and a very full life—I decided it was time. I was ready to start my degree once more.

Based on my business experience, I could have earned an MBA in a couple of years. But I didn't want it for the sake of creden-tials—I wanted it for the sake of my mind. I chose a degree in English Language and Literature, believing that mastery of language could help me master my responsibilities as a leader. After all, influential leadership is improved by linguistic per-suasiveness as well as personal example.

Over the next five years that it took to complete my stud-ies, I had two more children, became the European managing director and then global president of the company (responsible for markets in thirty-five countries), moved house four times, moved from the UK to the USA, and traveled to almost every market I was responsible for, some of them many times over. To keep the commitment I made of getting my degree, everything except the essentials had to be stripped away so that I could achieve my goals. My schedule included community and church responsibilities and a desire to balance work, life, and home against my school assignments. Not to mention a surgery somewhere in the middle of all of that which didn't allow me to sit in a chair for two weeks.

The pursuit of learning was a priority in every sense of the word, and the sacrifices it took to obtain it were enriching in ways that I never appreciated before. In spite of all the travel, extra children, promotions, and house moves, I was never late on an assignment, one of which I wrote while standing to recover from surgery.

My love for academia had expanded into a love for learning in all its forms. To grow our capacity for learning is to expand our horizons and our capacity for empowerment.

> Fear and hesitancy dissipate as understanding increases. In their place comes confidence, conviction, assurance, and belief.

THE PRIVILEGE AND RESPONSIBILITY OF EDUCATION

We've all heard it said that knowledge is power, but I'm not sure it's ever been truer than in this era of humanity. A few hundred years ago, people were born, lived, and died in the same place. Ethnocentricity—viewing another culture through the lens and biases of your own—was the standard, creating the notion of "barbarian" each time an explorer saw someone behaving differently than they expected. While there is no true justification for such behavior, ignorance pled a strong case for it. Now, thanks to the advancement of technology, the whole world is visible to us, and we are more informed and more opinionated than ever. With an increase of knowledge and awareness comes enlightenment and a long-overdue shift in what's possible.

Let's look for just a moment at the very essence of education. Step back if you will, from your current place in the world and let's view this from thirty thousand feet, so to speak. Knowledge has a transformative effect that ignorance and fear cannot stand. Education is a key component to improved tolerance and understanding, community development, and enriched skills that lead to new ideas, self-discovery, and self-improvement.

Ignorance gives way to fear and, without supplanting it, most certainly breeds destruction. In a very practical sense, this makes literacy, education for all, and access to higher education a desperate need for the progression of society.

Malala Yousafzai, the youngest Nobel Prize laureate and activist for female education, makes this single issue her way to counter the plague of terrorism. In as many avenues as possible, she is credited with the messages that education is power for women, and that power is what terrorists are afraid of. If we are to ensure equal opportunities for everyone, regardless of race, gender, social class, or any other bias, she insists, equal education is paramount.

In developing regions, education inequality often leads to child marriage, increased gender-based violence, and unnecessary maternal death rates. *Borgen* magazine, a publication devoted to the humanities and politics, further compiled the global benefits of education, including the following, rather impressive, list[29]:

> Improved health, lower crime, improved environment, gender equality, reduced fear and prejudice, improved tolerance and understanding, increased discipline, improved income, greater self-confidence, increased community involvement, enhanced critical-thinking skills and communication skills, a greater sense of purpose and accomplishment, and enriched skills that can lead to new ideas, self-discovery and self-improvement.

In detail, they note that the number one cause of poverty is lack of education, with the UN's Global Goals noting that 171 million people could be lifted out of extreme poverty if all children left school with basic reading skills. Countries with high literacy rates also have citizens with higher per capita income, signaling economic growth. By contrast, developing countries with a large number of people below the bread line usually have high illiteracy rates. Shamefully, there are 775 million illiterate adults in the world, and two-thirds of that number are women.

The benefits don't stop with literacy, either. The more educated a person is, the better their chance at higher-paid jobs. Statistically, according to the Global Partnership for Education, earnings increase by approximately 10 percent with each additional year of schooling.

---

29 Condensed from https://www.borgenmagazine.com/top-10-benefits-of-education/.

While economic benefits are easily connected with education, there are health benefits as well: children of educated mothers have a higher chance of living a healthier life, and their growth is less likely to be stunted by malnourishment. This is not only because better education leads to better choices, but because the higher income that results allows families to afford better food. Education also discourages crime, shaping people's understanding of right and wrong and obligation to society, and creating economic access that otherwise deters crime.

Most surprising, and perhaps most relevant for our time, environmental benefits come with more education as well. The more educated a population is, the more aware they are of environmental issues, which empowers them to act more responsibly in light of our global climate crisis. And, at its simplest beneficial level, green industries rely on educated people to further their sustainability efforts.

If you're reading this book from a place of access to education, turn inward for a moment to ask yourself whether you've taken full advantage of those privileges. In an age of learning, we are obliged to expand our capacity for knowledge however we can, both for our own benefit and for a greater societal hope for the future.

A WORD ABOUT PERSONAL RESPONSIBILITY

A number of years back, my brother and I were chatting with some friends after he came up to visit from New Zealand. He spoke of how beautiful the country was and how much he enjoyed living in *Aotearoa*, the Land of the Long White Cloud, as the Māori named it.

In response, our friend said, "It sounds beautiful. I'll tell you what. When I win the lottery, I'll come over to visit."

It's laughable, and we all knew that it meant he was giving up on the possibility. Yet this is how so many of us treat our dreams and heartfelt desires. *When the stars align…When the money is in the bank…When the opportunities come up…*When we have absolutely everything we need to qualify for that dream, then we'll take action. When we say this, we are lying to ourselves.

What these excuses say, essentially, is that we will leave our fate and future up to luck and chance.

While I believe in concepts like the Law of Attraction in their purest form, misinterpreting this principle by simply putting good feelings out into the universe has never been a strategy that I've seen delivered in the boardroom. Likewise, motivation, alignment with success principles, and a good mindset are important, but without a commitment to learning what's required for success, how will we know what path to take? Education, be it formal or informal, takes the guesswork out of growth.

The virtues of a disciplined heart and an educated mind are absolute necessities to achieve any vision. They are essential to our growth, and we must take personal responsibility to develop them.

With education, we position ourselves in such a way that we're ready to make the most of every opportunity that presents itself to us, and we equip ourselves to respond to every challenge.

Without an educated and informed mind, no amount of wishful thinking or strong desire can make your goals a reality. We discipline our hearts to take control of our emotions. To bridle them and focus them. Then we educate our minds to lighten the way that lies ahead.

ROADBLOCKS ON THE PATH TO KNOWLEDGE

The achievement of any dream requires wins, losses, pain, growth, and wisdom that we don't often anticipate. For many, the price required for victory is bigger than initially anticipated. So, they cut corners and choose the easier way. Like the undisciplined heart, they lay beneath the wind and appease whatever desires make life tolerable.

A strong character and realized dream do not reside along the path of least resistance, and anyone promoting otherwise is likely to be lining their pockets with your wishful thinking and hard-earned money.

As a young adult, the love I had for music grew into something of an early career. My best friend Richard and I both played jazz, traveling around the country playing music for radio, television, national festivals, and even for royalty a couple of times. We had a blast. We played together—he on the trumpet and me on the trombone, beginning in Dixieland bands and moving into big bands and jazz combo groups. We consumed the works of Dizzy Gillespie, Miles Davis, Charlie Parker, John Coltrane, J.J. Johnson, Curtis Fuller, Quincy Jones, and other jazz greats.

Here I was, this little white British kid who lived in New Zealand, obsessed with the African American jazz scene of decades ago. Sometimes, I would listen to these jazz masters and lament my heritage, wishing I was from the country and time of those

I revered. I looked at their ethnicity and saw a common thread and felt that I had been dealt a poor hand. With my white British history, I felt guilty by association for the creation of concert bands, excessive vibrato, and unsightly elbow bouncing that just wasn't hip.[30]

All this was a stark contrast to the cool jazz and cool players I loved. I felt, in contrast to these greats, like an impoverished vagrant out in the cold, looking enviously and hungrily through the restaurant window at the patrons inside enjoying a warm meal. I wanted in, and in my naivete, I thought that ethnicity was the ticket through the door. So, I lamented and wished. But I was white, not as cool, and from a different time. No amount of wishful thinking would change that.

The point of this strange admission is this: no matter how strong the desire, it will not establish a correct principle or lay a realistic foundation. This is critical to our pursuit of informal learning and education.

The objective of an educated mind is rooted in the commitment to a lifetime of learning, always expanding the horizons of knowledge, understanding, and experience. This leaves the bulk of our education as a self-directed effort, which creates a great deal of room for error.

An educated mind can inform the heart, and a disciplined heart can focus the mind.

---

30 Don't ask me about the elbow bouncing. I think it comes from the memory of a kid who moved his elbow in time to his incredibly exaggerated vibrato when he played the trumpet. It used to annoy the heck out of me unnecessarily.

In the way that we would deny an impulse in order to cultivate true desires, we must be careful as we pursue our own self-interest in the pursuit of self-education.

It is a paradox that we must deny ourselves in order to become our best selves, but it is one that has been embraced by wise voices for thousands of years. And in the spirit of that statement, to educate ourselves well, our wishful thinking cannot be fed like my foolish desires as a young jazz musician. We must anchor our learning in correct principles, reality, and truth, not feed pipedreams and impossibilities.

In a formal environment, we can expect that our educators have filtered through the information for us in order to present the most accurate and up-to-date perspectives. To some extent, we assume the same for on-the-job learning from our bosses and professional experts. But in any instance of self-education, we have to become our own filter, checking our self-interests at the door, for the same technology that gives us access to experts also gives us access to uninformed opinions, self-labeled gurus, and charlatans.

No court of law would establish a conviction on the voice of one witness, and neither should you. Think critically of the information you're receiving, and attempt to rule out self-promoters who just want your money. Especially in the age of social media, remember that the loudest voice with the biggest audience isn't always true and that self-education that serves our own biases or impatience will affirm wishful thinking, but will do little for our personal growth.

For all of the caution around self-education, it's a pursuit worth our constant devotion. Some of the best lessons I have learned came from outside the classroom. If we determine to draw from a range of perspectives throughout our lives, with a critical ear for expertise and an open mind to change our own entrenched beliefs, our capacity for knowledge will never stop growing.

FIGHTING AGAINST MEDIOCRITY

Though we are equal in value, we are not born equal in opportunities, nor do we all have the same natural abilities. This includes intellectual capacity. Thankfully, our natural abilities are only the start of our journey in life. We all have the ability to expand through study and experience, and to that experience comes wisdom, which can be finely tuned all the more as we pay careful attention to our conscience, desires, and vision for the future. It is an ever-building formula that we can manipulate to improve our intellectual state.

Let this serve as a warning against complacency, as well as motivation to push ourselves to greater levels of education over time. Don't let the fear of education or of failing at education put you off; remember that fear is a fruit of ignorance. As much as I desired the completion of my degree, I was terrified to return to the classroom after years away.

The first assignment for my English degree worried me so much that I questioned my aspirations. There is a vulnerability in being graded for our work that often affects our self-image. We're in the top, middle, low set, or simply failing. These turn into averages, which become labels, which define us throughout our time at school. Many of us go on to let those compartments define us for the rest of our lives. If we did okay at school, then it's okay to be middling at life later. Or if we failed academically, we might decide we simply aren't smart and will never be.

I found the opposite to be true. Whatever I thought about myself in grade school was no longer true of my adult self, and the grades I received on one assignment didn't determine the next. In fact, as an older student, I felt much smarter than I had been in school, simply because life had taught me, in essence, how to learn.

My degree predates my diagnosis, which means I was still battling my private demons along the way. In devouring books and mental health sources and expert knowledge about what might be wrong with me, I had been training myself to study on a much deeper level than I'd ever learned in school. It taught me discipline as well, which also made me a better student when the time came.

For as anxious as I was, my expectations and desire were stronger, and I thrived.

As with all other personal growth, it's okay to start small, especially in the face of fear and uncertainty. The challenge is to press against that fear, knowing that personal growth is worth the discomfort. The more we learn, the clearer our vision and choices become.

I'm not advocating for everyone to pursue doctorate levels of formal education—I certainly have not done so. But we all have an opportunity and responsibility to continue expanding to the next level throughout our lives, for as soon as we stop learning, we've condemned ourselves to mediocrity. Our commitment to this virtue—wherever we are in the context of learned skills—should be to constantly level up our game.

As a parent, you might study the developmental stages of

childhood to prepare for each new level of responsibility. As a leader, you might attend trainings to help you better relate to your team or understand your field. If you're already a doctor, you might stay abreast of the newest developments in your specialty. No role is too learned or too low to benefit from expansion. Take responsibility for that growth, never settling with past performance.

Ralph Waldo Emerson is often credited with having said, "This time, like all times, is a good one if we but know what to do with it." So many of us feel that same drive within us. We know there is something to be seized, an opportunity to be had, or a destiny to be realized. We want to run at it, but we don't know the path. Our time to act—to transform, to become, to improve—is now. But we need to know what to do with that time to make it so.

Knowledge is the starting point.

Fill your mind with learning. Pursue it. Develop a love for it. Curate a broad library of books, audiobooks, and podcasts, pursue higher education, and study under experts. Invest in formal enrichment whenever it makes sense. Validate everyone and everything, looking for evidence in the accomplishments and intellectual company that each of your sources keep.

The process of self-education is one that should continue throughout our lives, always striving to improve our understanding. However, no amount of discipline or education can eliminate all uncertainty. There will always be circumstances that we aren't prepared for, and new discoveries yet unknown. In those times, we must act in faith rather than sight—the next virtue that we will explore.

LEVEL UP YOUR LEARNING

Take stock of your education to this point. Start with the obvious—formal school and college experience. Training at work, courses, and certifications can come next. Then think of the other sources of learning you've pursued, from seminars to books to podcasts. Now, consider how you can level up. What sort of learning can you pursue next?

- If you have been facing a difficult obstacle and don't know how to overcome it, where can you go to find solutions?
- If you have great opportunities in your sight but don't quite have a grasp on them, what can you do now to better inform your path?
- Knowledge removes uncertainty. Are there areas in your life that cause anxiety and stress where new insights and education could provide relief? Where could you go to access this?
- From the lists provided in this chapter, what are some benefits you could enjoy from being better educated?

Remember, the empowering benefit of educating our mind is this: Learning is an active state driven by our personal commitment. We are taking control. We are not being tossed about in a sea of suffering, uncertain of what will befall us next. Knowledge is power, and you can have as much of it as you want.

Chapter 6

VIRTUE #3: NOURISHED FAITH

FAITH DETERMINES THE STEPS WE TAKE WHEN THE OUTCOME IS UNKNOWABLE

When my wife Kim went into labor with our first child, we excitedly and nervously rushed to the hospital. I wasn't prepared for what awaited, and Kim found the gas and air method of pain relief quite nauseating. She inadvertently ended up needing to deliver Ethan without anesthetic. As she neared the big moment when he was to arrive, she reached a point of fatigue and despair. "I can't do it," she moaned. This was my moment to step up and make a difference.

I took her by the hand. She squeezed it tightly, crushing my wedding ring into my fingers. *Man, that hurt!* Mistakenly, ignorantly—no, stupidly—I asked if she could let go for just a second while I took my ring off, as she was hurting my hand. "You think that hurts?" she said with a look that lacked any sense of empathy or tolerance at all. In fact, I think it was laced with undertones of aggression. Needless to say, she didn't let go, and to this day, I wonder if she squeezed just a little harder after that just to prove her point.

Bearing into the pain in my hand, I soldiered on. "Just one more contraction, Kim. You can do it," I said with as much encouragement and conviction as I could muster. She closed her eyes, focused, pushed, breathed through, and did great. But it wasn't over. There were more contractions ahead, so I continued with my strategy that seemed to be working.

"One more, Kim. You're nearly there. You can do it." She silently pressed forward with the delivery and soon enough, Ethan was born.

There were some complications in giving birth that required Kim to be taken into theatre for an hour or so after our son was born. As they wheeled her away, the nurses handed me my newborn, sleeping child.

I was standing in the middle of the room when they passed him to me. And there I remained, standing and afraid to move for the next hour in case he woke up.

"What on earth will I do if he wakes?" I thought to myself. I didn't want to risk it, so I feigned a preference to standing and waited desperately for Kim to return. It dawned on me in that moment that I had no idea what I had gotten myself into. I was beyond besotted with this little bundle of cuteness in my arms and at the same time, wholeheartedly terrified. Now, as the father of six boys and one girl, I am amused as I look back, and comforted that time marches forward in spite of our fears, leading us kindly to a better place.

As a brief aside, two weeks after Ethan arrived, still taking a great victory lap on my part as the overachieving husband in the delivery room, Kim broke the news: "Ben, do you remember when you were telling me 'just one more contraction, Kim—you can do it'?"

"Yes," I replied, waiting for her praise and thankfulness.

"Well, you were really annoying! Please don't do that next time."

Wait a second! What? I asked her why she didn't say anything during the labor and she explained. "It seemed that you really wanted to help, and I didn't want you to feel bad." I have always held my wife on a pedestal, but in that moment, it grew a few feet taller. Not only was she delivering our child without pain relief, but she simultaneously gave space for me to feel important and valued in spite of my own inadequacy and her frustrations and intense suffering. What can I say? She is simply inspirational.

I have learned through parenthood that most lessons are learned through loving practice. No parent knows everything required in their exciting new role, which is also the greatest responsibility of their lives. But love and care stimulate the mind to ask the right questions and inspire the courage to take the next step forward. That is how I grew as a father. And I'm pleased to say it didn't take long before I was in my element.

Life has a way of throwing things at us that demands a response outside of our skillset. And the response is often time-sensitive. Although the past can give some insights and people may provide support and encouragement, often there remains a space where we alone need to step up and lead out with faith.

What do we do when we can't access all the facts, when experience is limited, and the future is obscured from view? We keep moving forward. If it feels too much or too scary or too hard, we look a little closer to the next step and focus on that alone. Just one step. While there exists in our past evidence of our strength and reminders that the steps are manageable and that our struggles are only for a season, no struggle or victory is so great that it should be our last. With patience and courage, we take another step.

What if the fear and trepidation I felt as a brand new father had been the summit of my parental suffering? What would that suggest? Probably apathy, indifference, or personal absence. While they are unpleasant to endure, often the struggles we experience exist to educate, enrich, and expand us. With the right perspective, we can be strengthened by our past struggles, and this can empower us to not only endure, but to endure *well* the current challenges we face.

If we're going to look to the future, let it be to one of summits conquered and success well earned. Of realized dreams and rich rewards for hard work.

If we're going to look to the past, let it be to validate our strength and empower the next decisions we must make.

Life constantly requires that we give birth to newer versions of ourselves. Improved versions. The passage to this exciting, new world is also uncomfortable, unpleasant, and often difficult. But isn't it wonderful to know that our delivery isn't the pinnacle? Our purpose isn't found in the end of the ordeal, but in the new life it has created.

"We do not need and, indeed, never will have all the answers before we act...It is often only through taking action that we can discover some of them." —Charlotte Bunch

UNDERSTANDING THE ELEMENTS OF FAITH

Be it as individuals, groups or teams, or families: successful change, in any setting, comes when the status quo feels more dangerous or unacceptable than launching into the unknown. In that space, faith is required of us all. While there are religious or spiritual connotations with the word *faith*, please understand that faith is something that every human being possesses—religious or not—because it's what one has faith *in* that defines it as religious, not the faith itself. For the context of this book, I am not referring to religious faith, but the virtue we need when knowledge is incomplete or not enough.

By way of etymology, faith comes from an old French word, *feid*, meaning belief, trust, confidence, or pledge.

Faith includes, as a start, the expectation of a future or outcome that you currently cannot see. It could be the vision of a better version of yourself, or of some relief from adversity when none is in sight. Belief in that vision and a degree of hope that good things will come compels us to move forward, and faith gives us the strength to do so.

In a sense, every action you've ever taken is rooted in faith. Would a farmer plant a field without faith that it would yield a crop? Would a child ask something of their parents if they didn't trust it could be given? Would the student undertake a college degree without believing something better lay ahead because of it? We cannot know what the weather, our parents, or our education will actually bring, yet we press on with faith in an envisioned outcome.

There are some who feel it is an honest thing to give their doubts a prominent position, giving faith the second seat. They paint optimism as naïve or uninformed. But this is misplaced. Faith is most certainly a counterbalance to doubt, but giving our doubts and barriers strength is just as disempowering as leading with naiveté. Faith is an act of courage that is bolstered by knowledge rather than blissful ignorance.

At the same time, while faith can conquer our doubts, it doesn't necessarily eliminate them. Why? Because faith means we don't fully know the future.

We learn good farming techniques, trust our parents' character, and choose the path of education judiciously, not because we know the outcome without a doubt, but because we have a well-educated faith in potential. We look to the past for evidence of that potential, then expand our learning and action to direct the most reasonable path forward.

Austin Farrer, a twentieth-century theologian and scholar, described the marriage of faith and knowledge as this: "Rational argument does not create belief, but it maintains a climate in which belief may flourish."[31]

The poet Matthew Arnold admonished, "Faith is being able

---

31 Austin Farrer, "Grete Clerk," in Jocelyn Gibb, comp., Light on C.S. Lewis (New York: Harcourt & Brace, 1965)

to cleave to a power of goodness, appealing to our highest and real self, not to our lower and apparent self."[32]

Thus, we begin with a disciplined heart and an educated mind, then nurture faith as part of well-reasoned actions in service of our highest self.

THE UNCOMFORTABLE UNKNOWN

The vision, belief, and hope inherent in acts of faith compel us to act, at times with measured risk in light of the unknown. That risk only seems worth taking when present circumstances are worth sacrificing for the hope of a better outcome. Sometimes that excitement or discomfort comes to us apart from our own will, through adversity or opportunity, while other times we must step outside our comfort zone with intention.

For example, in a series of occasionally uncomfortable events that I couldn't help but embrace, I pursued—and won over—the heart of my future wife.

I met Kim in my twenties after I moved to the UK. She was the younger sister of a great friend (and now, even better brother in law), and after he moved away from home, I continued to go over to visit her instead. As our friendship blossomed, social norms sprinkled a seasoning of pressure. We had a lot in common, but she was about four inches taller than me. As our friendship turned to relationship, I would step onto the curb or a step to kiss her goodnight, to close the gap a little and draw her attention away from our height disparity.

---

32   Matthew Arnold, "Literature & Dogma," 1873

Every action you've ever taken is rooted in faith.

After more than twenty years of marriage, we can laugh now at the silliness of our concerns, but there was a good bit of social pressure on us. Even after she decided to go out with me, people couldn't wrap their heads around it. We worked in the same place, and one Friday night, with plans to go out, a co-worker tried to invite himself along. After leaving a few hints that a third wheel wouldn't be welcome, we finally had to say outright that we were a couple because it simply didn't register with him.

I was head over heels for Kim and believed our relationship to be possible. I didn't give room for my doubts and gave little room for hers. Sometimes, we simply have to take a leap of faith into the uncomfortable unknown in spite of what society tells us is safe and normal.

THE ELEMENT OF BELIEF

By its very nature, faith is not perfect knowledge. The process of empowerment is entangled with belief mixed with hope and doubt, trepidation, vision, and apprehension. Unfortunately, many of us wait for belief to emerge victorious. We simply don't trust that we are equipped for the unknowns that lay ahead.

I have now spoken to audiences in over thirty countries around the world, from small workshops to numbers in the thousands. In as many instances as I could, I have made this statement:

The biggest barrier to success, in life and in business, is the belief that we have in ourselves.

Each time, I ask for feedback, and each time the audience responds in unanimous agreement: the changes that we need to make for our businesses, for self-improvement, and to change our lives, are held back by a lack of belief more than any other obstacle.

Yet if we stick to what's safe—social norms, the known, or only doing what everyone else has done—we'll end up with the same banal and uninspiring results. I pursued my wife as the woman of my dreams, even though it went against social norms to say that I could because I didn't want a mediocre marriage with just anyone. I wanted an amazing life with her in particular.

Mediocrity is not enough for someone striving to be the best version of themselves. At front and center of exercising our faith in this capacity is to not surrender to our own self-protecting interests. If we constantly give in to desires for comfort, belonging, and ease, we will never be equipped to change. Transformation through faith requires us to feel the full weight of life's demands in order to respond effectively to them. We cannot live in a false reality and expect that path to take us to a better place. We must own everything about our present situation, and with that ownership, keep hold of a firm belief that we can navigate upwards to new heights. Of necessity, there must be some swimming upstream, going against convention, fighting against the status quo, and disagreeing with common opinion.

This will challenge the comfort of others around us, as well. That might manifest as disagreement, anger, and pushback, just as every great visionary has experienced. This should be a reassurance to us all, that it is normal and expected to find our next steps daunting and, at times, lonely. In these moments, when our belief is self-centric and we're not feeling up to the task, we're often right to waiver in our confidence. If we think we have to go it alone, we won't get far at all. Even when swimming upstream and feeling alone in our vision or pursuit of progress, we can tap into the strength of trusted others for the support and extra belief we need.

TRUST IN OURSELVES AND OTHERS

We rarely attain perfect, doubtless faith. It is a growing virtue, nurtured and developed over time from something small into something powerful. Along the way, doubt and fear—and apprehension and timidity—will coexist. That fear doesn't indicate a lack of faith. It simply means we are human, pursuing a path without complete knowledge of its trajectory.

There will be times when our own trust and belief falters beyond our ability to recover alone. In those times, trust in someone close to us can make all the difference.

For my twenty years of marriage, I have been able to rely on my wife's belief in me when my own was not sufficient. Her belief in what is right, and that doing what is right will bring evidence of change over time, has allowed me to move forward in faith even when I couldn't see those things for myself.

Early on in my career, working as a media manager for a direct selling company, my goal was to become their marketing manager for the European division. I reached out to my boss and asked if I could have the position. In response, he put the control in my hands with a trial of sorts. A product launch across our region was coming up with the company president, chairman, VP of global business, and VP of global marketing.

If I wanted to secure the role I sought, I would need to build relationships and show those people that I would be a valuable asset in the department.

I accepted the challenge and was even excited about my chances—until the executives came into town. They all worked in one wing in the corporate office in Texas. Needless to say, they were a tightly-knit group. Rightly or wrongly, it seemed to me that they treated my boss, who had his own lofty role in the company, as something of a gofer. As we traveled from place to place, he would be putting bags in the back of the car for them while they stood around chatting and drinking coffee.

They were nice enough, but I could get little more recognition from them than a nod or smile. My role wasn't even on their radar, so I certainly couldn't get any attention. Lying in the hotel bed with Kim, who had come along so I didn't have to drive the truck full of event materials myself, I bemoaned my fate. My chances of breaking into that group as nothing but a young minion were low.

At breakfast the next morning, she and I got our food and walked to a table just past the executives. On my way, I said good morning as always, and they acknowledged me, then carried on with their conversation. I sat down at the table feeling a little frustrated and expecting Kim to be right behind me, but instead, I saw her standing at their table.

As they came into earshot when I went back to retrieve her, she was saying this:

"All right, so here's the deal: the person that gets to Berlin last has to wear a dress on stage."

I was dumbfounded. What on earth was she doing, and how could I—

But they were laughing. Hysterically. Out came the American trash talk, and nothing was ever the same again. Not long after we packed up to leave for the next city, I started getting phone calls from them.

"Just curious, Ben. Where are you right now?"

"Ben, are you a fan of chiffon?"

"What kind of dress should we pick up for you tonight?"

None of us wound up actually wearing a dress, but from then on, we enjoyed a wonderful trip filled with banter, conversation, and camaraderie. My initial perceptions were wrong, and Kim opened the door to my opportunity. Ultimately, I got the promotion I was after, all thanks to the leap of faith that my wife was willing to take and that I was able to go along with.

Making a significant change is never easy, and it cannot be done in isolation. When we lack faith in ourselves, when we struggle to respond in line with a belief in our future selves, or when life has knocked us down too many times to believe that measured steps will create measurable outcomes, we must turn to someone else who can provide that belief for us.

Humility, then, becomes a key support for faith, reminding us again that we are part of the whole of humanity, and do not need to know or control everything around us in order to move on. We can humbly put our faith in those around us, trusting their judgment and belief in us, and return our focus to the future self that we're striving to be. In our response to the future values and strengths we hope to have, we can take action with confidence in the present.

Without that connection to a belief that's bigger than our own, we're on shaky ground for change. We need people in our lives who remind us of their unconditional love for us, no matter what choices we make. We must find these people, grow close to them, and whenever possible, be that person for others as well.

ACTION IN THE FACE OF THE UNKNOWN

As we evolve into who we're meant to be, there will be moments when our next step falls in the dark. We cannot wait until we know everything, or for all of the elements to line up to take the perfect shot on the perfect day in the perfect weather. That hesitancy is born of wishful thinking—the same kind that envisions a future free of stress in order to create happiness.

To lead with what we know, without letting what we *don't* know hold us back, requires courageous action. Indeed, action is often our best teacher.

As the managing director for a European business, my boss flew over from our California headquarters to meet with me. Again, though this time with a different company, a new product was about to launch, and he was preparing to travel around with me for the events. Before we left on the tour, he let me know that the chairman wanted to retire and promote him, my boss, from president and CEO to chairman. Plans were in place to look for a new president to fill the role that he would vacate, and he wanted to let me know to prepare for a new boss.

Out of curiosity and ambition, I thanked him for the heads-up and then asked him whether I could become the new president. "You're looking for a new president," I said. "Why not me? As long as Kim is willing to relocate to California, of course, I'd love the role."

My boss was surprised but willing to consider it, so our discussions began. In between speaking assignments for the launch events, we picked apart the business and discussed everything that we could. He asked about my approach strategically and my perspective on all kinds of issues. At the end of the brief tour, he offered me the job without a single formal interview. He simply told me there was an opening, and I raised my hand to ask for it.

The path to something extraordinary is traversed with small steps taken every day. I took a leap of faith and asked. I believed what could be, made a commitment to drive toward it, and then great things happened as a result. This has been true time and again.

In order for faith to grow, we must act. Whether the better version of ourselves is a great leader, entrepreneur, or a better mother or father, the starting point is in a decision right in front of us. Do we act now or not?

In a motivational environment, or when we hear an inspiring story, we often want to step out and do something big. We are uplifted by the idea of someone else's accomplishment and we want to follow in their footsteps. But for great things to be achieved in our own lives, we have to return to our own circumstances—regular day job, regular routine, regular things, often no longer surrounded by inspiration and excitement. So, we are then burdened with the mighty task of acting with faith, not in a singular, inspiring moment, but with the grind of the every-day, in repeated steps where growth starts out unseen but is happening, nonetheless.

Because we're in a lifelong pursuit of betterment, action cannot happen once and then give way to complacency in normal life. Character does not change with outbursts of occasional showmanship. Zig Ziglar famously emphasized this when he said, "Some people say that motivation doesn't last. Well, neither does bathing—that's why we recommend it daily." If we can cultivate faith in our futures through small but consistent steps, each achieved one after another, the fruits of what we believe to be possible will follow, and faith will grow along the way.

> The path to something extraordinary is traversed with small steps taken every day.

FAITHFUL ACCEPTANCE

The need for faith in our pursuit of empowerment applies not just to our consistent and proactive creation of a designed future, but also to our need for temperance and patient waiting while the day we've envisioned draws closer, and slowly, at that. The process of transformation is one drawn out over time, allowing certain elements of our lives to mature and develop even when we think we are sufficiently mature and developed. Understanding the leavening effect of time can be a faith-promoting power to us when circumstance seems determined to see us sink.

When heart.org recommends stress management techniques, they don't tell us to simply deal with what comes all at once, in its fullest measure. They ask us to break it down into manageable pieces.[33] You might change your breathing. Slow down and count to ten before speaking. Meditate. Sleep on things. If you're going to send an email in a moment of fiery indignation, leave it in the draft folder overnight instead. Walk away for a moment to adjust your mood. The most accomplished people break big problems down into smaller ones, then take them a step at a time.

This measure of acceptance is one that allows us to take the next right steps, even when we don't know how long it will take to get there or where "there" is at all. Nowhere is this more evident than in the process of grief.

A good friend of mine lost a loved one unexpectedly, and they were completely, understandably, devastated with grief. She explained the early days as overwhelming: "How could I manage the next fifty years of my life without seeing my best friend? The thought of it could send me catatonic."

But then, she explained that she learned to cope by taking it a day at a time: "I realized that I didn't need to deal with all fifty years at once. I just had to deal with today."

Acceptance of the struggle is about accepting our response to it. A measure of self-awareness can help us to face the reality of our faith or lack thereof, so that we may adjust accordingly.

These stories and messages that we tell ourselves can feed our insecurities and press us into resistance or allow us to accept the moment without losing faith for the future.

---

33 Heart.Org Stress Management, "3 Tips to Manage Stress," Accessed Online January 2020. https://www.heart.org/en/healthy-living/healthy-lifestyle/stress-management/3-tips-to-manage-stress.

From *I can't do this* to *I'll do the best I can.*

From *Everything is going wrong* to *I can handle this one step at a time.*

From *I feel helpless and alone* to *I can reach out and get help if I need it.*

From *I can't believe I screwed up* to *I'm human and we all make mistakes.*

If we need to develop greater faith in ourselves, we can begin by looking to past experience for evidence of progress.

There's proof all around us that we have done hard things over time, regardless of who we are and what we have achieved. Our job is to bring those achievements into view and hold them there, allowing those milestones to be built into something bigger.

> Acceptance of the struggle is really about accepting responsibility for our response to it.

THE FAITH OF HUMILITY

Over time, by circumstance or by choice, life may demand that we take larger leaps of faith. This faith will require complete surrender of our present selves in service of the future. We might need to let go of offenses or forgive someone where they have caused suffering. We might need to trust the direction a leader has given, though it feels radically different and overwhelming in its newness. We might need to move forward in crisis, not knowing how the outcome will unfold. In those times, such as Kim's intervention with the executives on our road trip, we can rarely go it alone.

When the Department of Trade and Industry showed up at my office with intent to shut us down (recall the story from chapter 2), as much as we asked them to inform us of their concerns, they were under no obligation to tell us. We did our work in the dark, attempting to respond without fully knowing what the future would hold. People came to me as the general manager, asking me if they were going to be able to pay their mortgage or feed their families, and I had to respond in a way that exercised faith in our ability to overcome—exercising confidence amidst a seemingly unwinnable circumstance.

Now on the other side of the struggle, that faith has become knowledge, and I'm pleased to say that we did win. We did everything required to transform, fight, and overcome, and the unbeatable odds were beaten. There was no prescribed path for change to follow at the time, the analysis of market-wide transformation has been the subject of much study since then, and I'm pleased to say that our path has been well-trodden.[34]

I have learned from this experience that personal change is a prerequisite of organizational change, but that organizational change requires a few extra layers.

The starting point was to create a sense of urgency that imposed a need for transformation. We didn't hide the urgency from our

34 John P. Kotter, "Leading Change: Why Transformation Efforts Fail," *Harvard Business Review*, 1995. https://oupub.etsu.edu/125/newbudgetprocess/documents/leading_change_why_transformation_efforts_fail.pdf.

people—and we needed to look out for anxiety, which is the counterfeit emotion of urgency.

We had a true and urgent need to make change, which everyone needed to see in order to inspire our steps into the uncomfortable unknown. We didn't know exactly what our arguments in court would be or what the internal change would require, but we knew the magnitude and the timeline. Everything had to be announced and executed before the court date.

Next, we needed to rely on the organization as a whole, not one single person. As humans, we are better able to make change within the construct of accountability and social responsibility to each other than we are on our own. The greater the cost of breaking the commitment, the more effective that social pressure is.

For example, in a field experiment done at a hotel, there was a 25 percent greater towel reuse rate amongst guests who committed to reuse towels during check-in and wore a "Friend of the Earth" lapel pin to signal that commitment.[35] Similarly, in the crisis I was navigating at work, we had to defer to our accountability to each other in order to maintain a complete, humble perspective and resolute commitment. For us, that looked like clearly defined roles of responsibility, transparency in communication, and regular team updates.

These new roles were the outcome of us creating a crisis team comprised of senior-level, experienced staff who could govern

35 Katie Baca-Motes, et al, "Commitment and Behavior Change: Evidence from the Field," *Journal of Consumer Research*, Volume 39, Issue 5, 1 February 2013, Pages 1070–1084, https://doi.org/10.1086/667226.

the transformation, with a clear and compelling vision of what that change would look like within a prescribed timeframe.

From there, the crisis team had to then empower others in the organization to make decisions and act on the vision. For this, we needed to create immediate wins.

Without an exact understanding of the ultimate outcome, there had to be a sense of achievement along the way. Nurtured and reinforced faith deepens our level of commitment and allows us to keep pressing forward into the unknown. This can be done with meaningful, timely, and regular feedback. Quick wins give immediate reassurance that we're on the right track and doing the right things. That gives fuel to bigger actions, which over time become entrenched within the organization.

We were birthing a new culture, not temporary behavioral change. And it was exciting.

The principles for personal change are the same as we seek to exercise faith in ourselves and make great change within. We need to establish a vision with a firm commitment to achieve it, and create a sense of urgency that teaches us to act on that vision now. We need to partner up—create a crisis team of sorts with people who have our best interests front and center, and share our goals and wins together to reinforce it all along the way.

Great personal transformation doesn't happen in a vacuum. It also doesn't happen in a moment. In life, we might need a crisis team of our own when a job is lost, a marriage is at risk, or we are grieving a death. When it feels like too much to handle alone, our trusted friends and advisors can help to provide perspective and accountability.

What is essential is the need to keep focused on your new behaviors once the crisis or transformation is over. Don't let complacency, victory, or the absence of crisis divert your attention from the new world you've created. Failure to do this will see behavioral or emotional erosion set in, and you will revert back to the former state.

THE JOURNEY OF A LIFETIME

Aristotle said this of the development of character: "It is our duty not simply to be functional, but to pursue excellence, and in order to achieve excellence in our pursuit of fulfillment, it requires a lifetime. One swallow doesn't make a spring, nor does a single fine day. Similarly, one day does not make a man blessed or happy."[36]

To that end, we should also consider the opposite: When we're wallowing in the mire of struggle or suffering, such a time does not define our entire lives. It is only a season.

Steps of faith towards progress and improvement lead us further away from the notion that happiness exists within a struggle-free bubble. Without this understanding, we might interpret struggle as us having gotten something wrong, or as reaching beyond our scope toward something we neither deserve nor can handle.

Mediocrity would have us stay in average jobs, be broken by broken marriages, be buried permanently in debt, and wind up forever lost in life. But signs and symptoms of broken relation-

---

36 *The Philosophy of Aristotle*, Published by Signet Classics, New American Library, a division of Penguin Group (USA) Inc., 2003, Introduction by Renford Bambrough, 1963, Afterword by Susanne Bobzien, 2011.

ships, debt, unfulfilling jobs, and a lack of direction in life are not in themselves signs of mediocrity or poor performance and should not be construed as such. They are simply a snapshot of a moment in time that tells the story of a thousand different interactions. And that snapshot can look very different in another moment in time down the road if we choose to apply ourselves to these virtues.

It is important to note here that struggle is not an indicator that we are out of our depth. Instead, we must welcome challenges as part of the journey toward a higher self. We must strive instead, with great faith, toward a future that we cannot yet see, but that we believe will come to fruition over time, with great effort and support from those who love us.

I feel as I write this, the great need to reach out to the reader who may be struggling to have sufficient faith in their future or themselves, hug the life out of them, and say, "Don't you give up!"

You're stronger than you know. Your future is brighter than you can imagine.

I mentioned early on that bipolar disorder is a gift. And it really is. Something that takes you to the absolute limits of your mind and emotions, tearing at you and your sense of who you are, developing a heart that is well acquainted with pain. Enduring this over time brings a sensitivity to the suffering of others that is unique. I treasure that sensitivity. It could not be born any other way. It came at a price. And surely such suffering on my part can be worth it if it enables me to help others who struggle to see the light ahead and give them courage to take the next step forward.

NURTURE YOUR FAITH

Consider a precarious situation that you're facing—a decision to make, a crisis to resolve, or a barrier to overcome. Are the potential outcomes of your next steps known? Has the unknown held you back?

Give yourself some time to reflect on what's needed to move forward in that situation, and identify the areas of faith that you might nurture to do so. As you reflect on your own personal empowerment journey, ask the following questions:

- In what ways can I act in faith in spite of present doubts and fears?
- Who can I trust and involve in my journey that will give me added strength?
- In what ways can I be a strength to others?
- What role does time play in this process?
- If the transformation required seems too much, what is the next small step I can take now?
- How can I build a greater sense of personal accountability into my transformation journey?

Chapter 7

VIRTUE #4: WELL-PRACTICED PATIENCE

AFTER THE INEVITABLE PASSAGE OF TIME, THE ONLY THING WE KEEP IS THE PERSON WE HAVE BECOME

The case for patience is strong, showing itself time and again to be integral to all growth on planet earth, from the biggest tree to the smallest step toward a stronger character. Patience is not only essential to our pursuit of all virtues, but it is a virtue to be pursued in itself. For it's not necessarily adversity alone that shapes us or simply our immediate response to it. All too often, the real test is the duration of adversity and the required response it asks of us in time.

Julius Caesar knew this when he said, "It is easier to find men who will volunteer to die than to find those who will endure pain with patience." But the ever-inspirational Helen Keller had a different take: "We could never learn to be brave and patient if there were only joy in the world.

To her, a positive attitude created feelings of privilege rather than disadvantage, and she certainly knew how to endure pain with patience.

Helen's story is a well-known example of the relationship of time, patience, and the development of character. The two others we'll review in this chapter—Beethoven and John Milton—are also known and used as examples, perhaps to the point of cliché. But as we compare and contrast their scenarios within the context of our seven virtues, fresh and valuable insights as to how and what we learn through time are revealed. For those who will review old stories with new eyes, there is an important message pending.

> "The man who is a master of patience is master of everything else."—George Savile

HELEN, LUDWIG, AND JOHN

In *The Story of My Life*, Helen Keller gave voice to some of the difficulties she experienced growing up both blind and deaf. At times, her life was silent, aimless, and dayless, without any concept of relationship, family, or emotion. Of this unimaginable sense of isolation, she wrote, "In the valley of twofold solitude, we know little of the tender affections that grow out of endearing words and actions and companionship."

Helen moved through life without any means of interaction with the world, and therefore no way to understand it, until her patient and persistent teacher, Anne Sullivan, finally unlocked language for Helen. By signing the word W-A-T-E-R into one hand while simultaneously pouring cool running water on the other, Helen made the connection and her world was changed.

Finally having a name for that wonderful cooling *something* that had sustained her life, Helen later wrote, "awakened my soul and gave it light, hope, joy, and set it free."

With a new world quite literally at her fingertips, a great task lay ahead of her—not only to do the difficult work of coping with her adversity, but to change herself in response. From the first time she slipped into the sea and went under water, to being caught climbing a tree as a thunderstorm rolled in without any way for her to know, every interaction with the world around her required patience to understand and survive. Yet, no matter how painful the process, she relayed every event as rewarding in its own way. Of this, she wrote:

> "Sometimes, it's true: a sense of isolation enfolds me like a cold mist as I sit alone and wait at life's shut gate. Beyond, there is light, and music, and sweet companionship, but I may not enter. Fate, silent, pitiless, bars the way. Feign, I would question his imperious decree, for my heart is still undisciplined and passionate…Then comes hope with a smile and whispers, 'There is joy in self-forgetfulness.' I try to make the light in others' eyes my sun, the music in others' ears my symphony, the smile on others' lips my happiness."[37]

Helen Keller knew better than most that there is struggle woven into the fabric of life itself, sometimes irretrievably so. With no way to alleviate her circumstance, she could only face it, endure it with patience, and grow as a person in light of it.

The example of Beethoven gives us another perspective of enduring adversity, this time as much rooted in knowing as

37 Helen Keller, *The Story of My Life*. Restored edition, edited by James Berger, 2004 Modern Library Paperback Edition, by Random House Inc.

Helen's was in the unknown.[38] It wasn't until his mid-twenties that he began to lose his hearing, after having composed and performed music since he was a young child. At twenty-six, he wrote that he was hearing a buzzing and ringing all the time. At thirty, he wrote to a friend that he had to "get very close to the orchestra to understand the performance," and that speaking voices were becoming difficult to hear. By the time he wrote his Fifth Symphony in his mid-thirties, he was completely deaf.

As the world he knew slowly slipped from his grasp, Beethoven stopped going to social gatherings, fearing that he couldn't tell anyone about his affliction. The loss of hearing for a composer felt like the loss of identity as well. He wrote to a close friend, "If I belonged to any other profession, it would be easier. But in my profession, it is a frightful state."

He tried all kinds of remedies to subvert his hearing loss, including strapping wet bark to his upper arms until it dried out. This obviously didn't cure his hearing loss, though it did keep him away from his piano with blisters all over his arms. He tried wearing primitive hearing devices and used amplifiers and trumpets on his piano. The less the remedies worked, the more he learned to continue composing in spite of his affliction.

In Beethoven's early work when he could hear the full range of frequencies, he made great use of higher notes in his compositions. As time progressed and his hearing regressed, his

---

38   Classic FM Composers, "So if Beethoven was completely deaf, how did he compose?," ClassicFM.com. Accessed Online January 2020. https://www.classicfm.com/composers/ beethoven/guides/deaf-hearing-loss-composing/.

Donato Cabrera, "The Whole Story of Beethoven's Deafness," Medium.com, January 2018.

https://medium.com/@CASymphony/the-whole-story-of-beethovens-deafness-30944c94143.

works used lower notes more and more. We see him adjusting his compositions to what he could hear, rather than amplifying his hearing to what he already understood. For much of his life, he had been a composer. Now, he was a deaf composer, and he had to adapt to that.

Fascinatingly, much later in life, higher notes returned to his compositions. This was not because he returned to his earlier methods of composition, and it was certainly not because he regained his hearing. Rather, his approach to his circumstances evolved completely, and his musical compositions came to accommodate his imagination rather than his hearing or hearing loss.

The works he completed in total deafness include his Ninth Symphony, which was reviewed more in the years after its premiere than any of his previous compositions. It is considered an autobiographical narrative of tragedy and joy, indicating something of a triumph over his deafness.

What must he have gone through as a great composer to finally come to a place of acceptance with permanent hearing loss? What patience must he have developed to adapt his life to personal circumstances that he could not change—no matter how desperately he wanted to? What bliss must he have felt when he could eventually relinquish the restrictions he placed on composition and trust more in his imagination and the full weight of his genius?

A similar struggle is mirrored in another classic creative, for nearly as tragic as a great musician going deaf is a great poet going blind. John Milton, the seventeenth-century English poet, was recognized for *Paradise Lost* and ultimately as one of the greatest poets of his day.[39] And he, too, gradually lost his key sense later in life.

Having spent some time as a writer and poet with full use of his vision, it began to deteriorate into adulthood. In one of his later poems, Milton expressed deep consideration for a life spent half in blindness and half with sight: "When I consider how my light is spent, Ere half my days, in this dark world and wide…Doth God exact day-labor, light denied?"

Recognizing his higher calling to serve his God in spite of adversity, he continued: "But patience, to prevent that murmur, soon replies, 'God doth not need either man's work or his own gifts; who best bear his mild yoke, they serve him best.'"

Having found something greater than himself to be his focus, he had incredible vision in spite of being blind, writing some of his greatest work amidst his greatest challenges. Likewise, Beethoven overcame isolation and hidden struggles, frightened about losing his identity within his adversity, but going on to compose some of his most complex masterpieces. And Helen Keller, who was born into total communicative isolation, persevered alongside her teacher to find that true joy is appreciated because of suffering, not in spite of it. She was able to find good in every situation, no matter how terrifying, recognizing that each circumstance is designed to grow her into a better person.

Each of these disabilities were chronic, enduring for many years, if not all of their lives. They had to surrender, adapt, and even

---

39 George B. Bartley, M.D., "The Blindness of John Milton," *Mayo Clinic Proceedings*, April 1993, Volume 68, Issue 4, Pages 395–399. https://www.mayoclinicproceedings.org/article/S0025-6196(12)60139-6/fulltext.

embrace their conditions in order to step into their highest selves. As a consequence, their talents seemed to amplify.

While these are among the greatest of humanity, demonstrating virtue and talent beyond comprehension, they provide more than an example on a pedestal. Their stories give us a rare look into practical ways to develop patience as an intentionally developed virtue. In this chapter, we'll consider the consistent roles that imagination, surrendering of an existing identity, and deep connection to support systems play in the cultivation of patience.

IMAGINE A FUTURE WORTH WAITING FOR

The old, tongue-in-cheek prayer, "Lord, give me patience, but give it now," highlights our universal desire for patience, as well as our struggle against it. We spent a fair amount of time on the concept of patience in chapter 2, but what does it mean to develop patience as a virtue in itself?

Patience is more than just the will to allow time to pass. It is the art of responding well as time passes through us. By definition, it is an active participation with the events that come to us over time—certainly not to be confused with the counterfeit emotion of complacency. Patience requires endurance, submission, and humility. It is the resolve that moves us forward toward our vision while bearing with endurance the adversity we are called to bear. Without a vision, it's difficult to appreciate the meaning along the way.

John Milton's vision was of his broader task on this earth. Focusing on it drove him to endure well that which was presented to him. He couldn't go back to his God with the excuse that he lacked the sight to do what he was called to do. The image of him standing honorably before God, void of excuses, drove him even further toward his purpose than he'd been able to achieve in earlier years.

Beethoven spent years adapting to the familiar as best he could, but at some point, his imagination took over more fully, and that's when he created some of his best work. In contrast, Helen Keller embraced the interplay of a life comprised of joy and struggle—to let the light in others' eyes be her sun and the music in other people's ears be her sound. Her imagination created worlds that she'd previously been denied.

All three took different paths, but all share a common thread in the development of their patient progress: Imagination. Imagination developed patience and provided solutions.

Patience is more than just the will to allow time to pass. It is the art of responding well as time passes through us.

Much more recently, neuroscientist Adrianna Jenkins and postdoctoral researcher Ming Hsu used brain scans to find that imagination is a pathway toward patience.[40] To demonstrate this potential, they designed studies that showed patience in action.

In one scenario, they offered participants $100 tomorrow or $120 in thirty days. In another, they shaped the offer in a sequence: $100 tomorrow *and nothing later*, or nothing tomorrow *and $120*

---

40 University of California-Berkeley Haas School of Business, "Be more patient? Imagine that," ScienceDaily, April 2017. https://www.sciencedaily.com/releases/2017/04/170404160028.htm.

in thirty days. With 122 participants who were presented with both framings of the options, more of them chose the delay, and with stronger preference when the option was presented as a sequence. In another round, a different set of participants made their choice based on one frame.

In each of the results, participants who chose the sequenced framing reported that they imagined the consequences of their choices more than the others did. One participant said, "It would be nice to have $100 now, but $20 at the end of the month is probably worth it, because it's a week's gas money." When broken down into sequences (now…and then), they were able to utilize their imaginations and exercise a greater sense of patience.

Remarkably, by envisioning a preferred outcome before acting on an impulse, patience is increased *without* reliance on increased willpower. The study notes, "Whereas willpower might enable people to override impulses, imagining the consequences of their choices might change the impulse…People tend to pay attention to what is in their immediate vicinity, but there are benefits to imagining the possible consequences of their choices."

The examples from Milton, Beethoven, and Keller demonstrate how grit and skill and natural determination are only pieces of the puzzle. More directly, each of them engaged their imaginations at some level, not simply enduring, but enduring well—to the achievement of incredible outcomes that have inspired generations since.

We, too, can think creatively and expansively to forge a new path through the struggle, rather than willing ourselves through with brute force. And, just as Jenkins and Hsu broke their experiment into sequences to engage imagination, we can endure lasting adversity by breaking our tasks down to moments.

An extreme but successful example is the twelve steps for Alcoholics Anonymous. In these instances, people are biologically detached from their willpower with a significantly compromised ability to choose. Yet when they break their life down into sequences of choices, one day at a time, they are able to engage their imaginations sufficiently to envision achievable success. *In this day, this hour, this moment, I can see myself making it to the other side.*

PROMPTS TO INSPIRE IMAGINATION AND SHAPE VISION

- What are our challenges, and what can we become as a consequence of them?
- What can we learn that will turn great struggle into great victory?
- How can we see beyond the barriers that hold us back?
- How can these barriers become the framework to shape the great work of our lives?

STOP ATTEMPTING TO REVISE REALITY

In our impatience, it's difficult to acknowledge or accept the barriers around us—health, addiction, mental well-being, loss, finances. Yet when we refuse to accept reality with patient endurance, we are unable to be present in our experience.

Every game of basketball has a court with boundary lines that cannot be crossed. Every athlete on a track has a line that defines their track. Every competitive swimmer has a lane to stay within. These parameters do not restrict the game, but rather create it. Barriers and boundaries make the game possible. If we refuse to accept those lines of demarcation in our own lives, we cannot overcome the challenges set forth for us.

What if Beethoven had refused to accept his hearing loss? What if Helen Keller had refused to accept a reality bigger than what she could sense? Or if Milton refused to acknowledge his path as a writer without sight? Some of the greatest, most inspiring compositions of our time would be lost to pointless suffering.

If you find it difficult to imagine their refusal to accept such tangible and undeniable realities, consider that we do it all the time. From a very basic starting point, why do we get stressed while stuck in traffic jams, even though there is nothing to be done about it? Because we refuse to accept the reality of our present situation. No matter how frustrated I get with the people around me, it doesn't make traffic move any faster.

Resistance to reality is the very basis of stress as we try to control things that we have no power over. Acceptance of reality allows my stress to diminish, which frees my mind up to be more imaginative and creative within the parameters I've been given on that road at that moment in time.

BRING YOUR IDENTITY BACK TO THE PRESENT

Breaking down the steps toward an outcome and creating a sequence that we can imagine overcoming helps us drive forward even beneath enduring struggle. But when we are evaluating performance, progress, and rate of change along that path, we cannot focus on outcome alone. Rather than measuring against the person we ultimately want to be, we must acknowledge the person that we are becoming.

Unfortunately, we often get lost in a mix of past and future states, sparking the moment of identity crisis we see in Beethoven's fear of losing his career. What he had done in the past had come to define his entire sense of self. But that's not the meaning of *identity* at all. The word itself is derived from the Latin *identitas*, meaning being, and *identidem*, meaning repeated. Your identity, then, is literally your repeated state of being.

Our habits, not our past or future, shape who we are.

In *Atomic Habits*, James Clear unpacked our often backward thinking around the formation of these habits. He noted three areas of change that we attempt to start from: outcomes, processes, and identity. Too often, when we're trying to change the habits in our lives, we start from the outside and work inward. We drive toward an outcome, which Clear says is the wrong way to go about it. The devotion is short-lived because it hasn't been assimilated with our identity.

When what we're doing resonates with who we are, then the behavior remains consistent over time. And here lies one of the many paradoxes of character development. We speak of vision and the need for clarity and faith in our future, yet to achieve it, we must see it, put a pin in it so to speak, and then get focused, not on the future, but in the present moment by habit-stacking aligned improvements with current behaviors. As Richard G. Scott once said, "We become who we want to be by consistently being who we want to become each day."

As much as we try to make it so, our identity is not tied to our professions or our infirmities or our circumstances, but to the beliefs and actions that shape us in the midst of those factors. When identity seems lost and belief is in crisis, our next steps matter; we can decide the type of person we want to be, then prove that we can be that person with small, repeated wins over time. Not only does this anchor our beliefs in what's possible, but our repeated actions literally become our present identity.

If we can start by changing our sense of identity in this way first, working from the inside out, then we create something lasting. This is true of all behaviors, not the least of which is patience. We are shaping our identity with every habit sustained over time, turning ourselves into that great creative work that will echo through the ages.

Our habits, not our past or future, shape who we are.

CONNECTION KEEPS US GOING

Another shared trait between the three greats we've analyzed here is the need for connection with others. Milton and Beethoven kept their secrets for some time, afraid for the world to know of their struggle, while Helen suffered in silence until Anne unlocked the gift of communication within her. The more patience they expressed with their purpose and journey, the better they were able to reconnect with the world around them—and ultimately reach us all.

So much of the weight of adversity is held up in isolation. There is great vulnerability in opening up to someone else and sharing the struggle with them, and vulnerability is a lifeline in the midst of enduring adversity. Yet so many of us choose to suffer in silence. What is it that causes so many to put their suffering into "airplane mode" and go radio silent? I think the imposter syndromes talked of earlier play a part, but so too do fear, worry, insecurity, doubt, concern for others, uncertainty, selflessness, and a host of other natural emotions that make us human.

In spite of the perceived risks, I wonder how many more solutions we would find if we were able to be open and transparent about our struggles with one another. How much more patient would we become by bringing our present worries out into the open? After all, when all we have is our own negative self-talk and limiting beliefs to listen to, our frame of mind is compromised, creating the greatest risks of all.

When we pull someone else into the equation, relying on their rational thought, encouragement, and love for us, our patience develops all the more.

PATIENCE IN CHOSEN ADVERSITY

When the necessity of patience is not imposed on us, the quality develops in a very different way. The patience that Helen Keller demonstrated was born out of necessity, while her teacher Anne Sullivan demonstrated a similar lifelong patience born out of love and choice. Her desire to serve, throughout many years of her life, came from a patient willingness to serve her friend. Both love and necessity can nurture the same virtue through very different mechanisms.

For both women, external circumstances were not going to change. They were simply motivated in different ways to embrace those circumstances with great imagination for a potential future, a deep sense of internal change and identity development, and an enduring, vulnerable connection to each other.

Anne Sullivan's patience was just as virtuous as Helen's, reflected in Helen's affections toward her. In her book, Helen said this of Anne:

> "My teacher is so near to me that I scarcely think of myself apart from her. How much of my delight in all beautiful things is innate, and how much is due to her influence, I can never tell. I feel that her being is inseparable from my own, and that the footsteps of my life are in hers. All the best of me belongs to her—there is not a talent, or an aspiration or a joy in me that has not been awakened by her loving touch."[41]

Anne and Helen were so intertwined in their experience and their work that Helen couldn't see where one began and another ended. Anne's love for Helen and her vision of a possible future engaged her imagination and fueled her own patience, which ultimately empowered Helen to find the highest version of herself.

Both love and necessity can nurture the virtue of patience.

PATIENCE IS NOT DEVOID OF EMOTION

We often think of patience as "this too shall pass." Take a deep breath and ignore it until it goes away. But true patience is

---

41 Helen Keller, *The Story of My Life*. Restored edition, edited by James Berger, 2004 Modern Library Paperback Edition, by Random House Inc.

exercised proactively, for as long as the circumstance endures. Sometimes, in our connection with others, this proactivity brings us into a trial of our choosing.

One of the most traumatic experiences of my life, which demanded from me the greatest test of patience in my life, was seeing my father go to prison. This was difficult not simply because he went to prison, but because I, with my brother, initiated the process.

When I was twenty-two, I took a one-way ticket and fifty pounds with me from New Zealand to the UK, with the hopes of sparking some kind of relationship with my father after years apart. When I got there, I discovered serious misconduct on his part, and I knew he wouldn't initiate retribution for it on his own. Out of love for him and a desire to see him get his life back on track, I got the police involved and facilitated the investigation that ensued.

This process came from both love and necessity.

With no money, a part-time job, and if you recall, having recently been kicked out of university and broken up with by my girlfriend, I was left with absolutely nothing. I was on the other side of the world from the family I'd grown up with, and no one to open up to about it at all. I couldn't even open up to myself about it. Verbalizing the magnitude of the situation, even as a cohesive thought in my head, was too much to fully confront for a great deal of the process.

It felt like an eternity before the investigation was completed and he was arrested. Knowing how the policed turned up at his door, how his time would be filled with interrogation, and seeing his world come undone was heartbreaking, and even more so because I felt like I had put him there.

As a consequence of my involvement, I was to be a witness in the courtroom, further embedding the pain that came from initiating the process. On the day of the court case, my brother and I arrived early at the Crown Court in Chester, England. We were given a tour of the courtroom so that we could see where the judge and jury would be, where we would be, and where my father would be sitting just a stone's throw away.

Then we were led to a waiting room, where we sat in silence until our names were called over a speaker. Our hearts ached with a suffering that's difficult to express in words, pounding with anxiety over the unknown of the testimonies to come. But before any of the proceedings could begin, an official came into the room and whispered something to the court official waiting with us. Then they broke the news that our father had a heart attack the night before.

Conflicting emotions swirled about. I loved my dad but hated what he had done. I impatiently wanted the process to be over, for him to be in prison and for this to be done. Now he was in the hospital. I resented that but then felt terrible that I did. I didn't want him in the hospital or prison. Yet the hospital was a good place for him to be and so was prison. Talk about an emotional mess.

After another stretch of sleepless months, the next hearing was scheduled. Once again, we were given the tour. Once again, we waited for our names to be called. We were finished at about 4:30 that afternoon, then went back to our hotel room to rest for a moment. Before we knew it, it was seven the next morning and time to leave for the second day in court. At the end of the day, we told ourselves the same thing—we'll rest for a moment and then unwind for the evening. Yet again, we were so completely drained that we awoke at seven the next morning.

After the judgment and sentencing, my life carried on while my father's remained in stasis. He was in prison when I got married. He was in prison when my first child was born, and for a number of years thereafter.

While I once again lived my life with an absent father, I could see bits of him in my own reflection, as well as in some of my interests and mannerisms. I would run into people who knew my father, and I would brace for what came next, not sure if the conversation was going to turn toward his business successes or to something more dubious. It became a question of identity, unsure of what to make of my own name.

It forced me to dig deeper, to really understand my personal identity both then and who I wanted to become. I had to turn the name of Woodward into something of my own making. I needed to make sense of the feelings swirling within me, to put the negative emotions in their proper place, and to build an appropriate relationship with him moving forward.

Remember, the goal is progress—not perfection.

It took a great many years to try to understand, dissect, and be changed by this odd and often painful relationship with my dad. We are still not as close as I'd envisioned we'd be back when I was a naïve kid traveling by plane to the UK. He's still a closed book, but it's more than the relationship with his handwriting in the occasional letters I received as a young child.[42]

Some of this struggle in the early years when my dad was absent was imposed on me, while the latter half of our struggles were self-imposed by my proactivity. I led the charges. I testified against him in court. I drove him to the courthouse to be sentenced. These were horrible experiences that, while not my fault, were at my initiation.

The waters of an ongoing relationship were murky. Like some kind of contemporary, unstructured dance, it required stepping forward and moving back, making commitments and then recommitting to them time and again. It taught me patience, not in a sense of enduring the passing of time, but enduring it well. It forced me to confront the events in front of me and find value in them, even when they were painful, then to ask what life might require of me in light of them.

If those events had control over me, they would certainly have shaped me into something I don't want to be. Patience requires action, not complacency.

As I grew toward values of love, forgiveness, and understanding, I could no longer hold on to the resentment and hurt that were very real, but not worth cultivating. If I had any hope of growing beyond childish desperation, I could neither be passive nor unforgiving. We all reach this point of decision between the uncomfortable path of pain and the impulse to turn away.

---

42 It's an odd side note, but handwriting is so unique isn't it? It's like a fingerprint, or a tone of voice. So a child getting a handwritten letter from a very absent father made it something uniquely special. I bonded with his letters in such a strange way.

When we lean into patience, enduring the reality in front of us to reach the virtues ahead, the reward is greater than the cost.

PATIENCE ON YOUR PATH

In the Shakespearean play *Othello*, we are admonished in our impatience and inaction: "How poor are they that have not patience! What wound did ever heal but by degrees?" Consider the circumstances you've been impatient with recently. Write out the nature of the struggle, and what's truly needed in order to overcome it, giving yourself more realistic expectations and a more intentional path forward.

Ask yourself the following questions:

· What role does your imagination currently play in your view of the future?
· How does your imagination impact your choices today regarding your priorities and potential?
· How can you engage your imagination to create a brighter future for your life, business, career, or relationships?
· What are some baby steps you can take to move progressively towards this brighter future?

Chapter 8

VIRTUE #5: A LIBERATED PAST

SHACKLING OURSELVES TO THE PAST LIMITS OUR REACH INTO THE FUTURE

In 2007, an eighteen-year-old Iranian boy named Abdollah Hosseinzadeh was stabbed and killed in a street brawl by an acquaintance who had played football with him. Tragically for Abdollah's mother, Samereh Alinejad, this was her second son lost, with her youngest dying in a motorbike accident at the age of eleven. In her grief, she was justifiably furious at the injustice of another great loss.

For seven years, Balal, her son's accused and convicted killer, remained in prison, awaiting the date of his execution. For those seven years, the grief of a lost child plagued Abdollah's parents.

In Iranian custom, culture, and law, Abdollah's father, Abdolghani had the power to overturn the death penalty if he so chose. It would not relinquish prison time, but simply give him the option to determine the finality of the retribution. In an expression of love and devotion to his wife, Abdolghani relinquished this responsibility entirely to her—and she saw no pathway toward forgiveness. She was determined that Balal would hang.

Leading up to the date of the execution, however, Alinejad began to experience vivid dreams in which her son came to her, asking her not to take revenge. Quoting her statement to *The Guardian*, she said, "Two nights before that day, I saw him in the dream once again, but this time he refused to speak to me."[43]

The night before the execution, she couldn't sleep. She told her husband that she couldn't imagine forgiving the man for what he'd done, to which he replied, "Let's just look to God and see what happens."

In the early hours of the morning, a crowd gathered to witness the execution. The process included a recitation from the Quran, while the blindfolded young man stood on a chair with a rope around his neck and his hands tied behind his back. Regardless of his crime, the scene was overwhelming. In the final moments, Balal cried out to Alinejad for forgiveness, if not for him, then for the sake of his parents.

Surprising everyone, likely herself as well, Alinejad walked up to the boy, and rather than exercising her right to push the chair away herself, slapped him hard across the face.

"After that," she recalled to *The Guardian*, "I felt as if rage had vanished within my heart. I felt as if the blood in my veins

43 Saeed Kamali Dehghan, "Iranian mother who spared her son's killer: 'Vengeance has left my heart'" *The Guardian*, April 2014. https://www.theguardian.com/world/2014/apr/25/interview-samereh-alinejad-iranian-mother-spared-sons-killer.

began to flow again. I burst into tears and called my husband up to remove the noose."

That moment of mercy, from a mother to the criminal who murdered her son, spread around the world. She became a hero, recognized in Istanbul as mother of the year, interviewed by many, and spoken of worldwide as a figure of inspiration.

When asked what lessons she hoped others would learn, she said, "For young people not to carry knives when they're going out…" But there was something much deeper that the incident conveyed. Of forgiveness, she said this: "All these years, I felt like I was a moving, dead body. But now I feel very calm. I feel that I'm at peace and that vengeance has left my heart."

Of necessity, if we are to transform into our greatest potential, we cannot hold on to the past. Whether it is mistakes we have made or hurt that others have caused, or even a sense of bitterness around opportunities or good fortune lost, we must let go of what holds us to the past or our reach into the future will have limits. Forgiveness of others, relinquishing disappointment in our past, and withholding prolonged self-judgment is paramount for us to have an unfettered and totally liberated future.

"Forgiveness is not an occasional act; it is a constant attitude."—Martin Luther King, Jr.

UNDERSTANDING FORGIVENESS

Is forgiveness an emotion, a behavior, or some combination of the two? What does it mean for our treatment of the person who has committed the offense?

Etymologically, "forgive" comes from the old English word *forgiefan*, meaning to give up, allow, remit, or pardon. Broken down further, *for* and *give* holds pardon in one half and remittance in the other, as the prefix *for* typically means away, opposite, or completely.

When seeking to forgive, we cannot go about it halfheartedly. To truly forgive, the debt or offense is pardoned completely and absolutely. Like the Iranian mother in an impossible circumstance, we must learn to abandon completely our desire for revenge when mercy needs to be served.

We must also accommodate forgiveness as a process rather than an event, and often one that must be repeated over and over again. Rarely can we make the decision to forgive and find that it has been completely let go. C.S. Lewis once said, "The real trouble about the duty of forgiveness is that you do it with all of your might on Monday, then find out on Wednesday that it hasn't stayed put and must be done all over again."[44]

In 1985 at the University of Wisconsin-Madison, researchers hoped to find some scientific outcomes from forgiveness—but, being good scientists, they needed to first define it as completely as possible. Looking across ancient literature to Jewish, Confucian, Buddhist, Christian, Muslim, and Hindu faiths, as well as modern philosophical writings, a common theme emerged: when unjustly treated by others, a person forgives by struggling to abandon resentment and offering the beneficence to the unjust person or people.

"Forgiveness, we saw, is a part of mercy. So it can appear to come

---

44   C.S. Lewis, *The Collected Letters of C.S. Lewis Volume III*, HarperOne, June, 2009.

from a position of weakness, as the unjustly treated person offers the olive branch. Yet forgiveness is anything but weak, because the forgiver is not condoning, excusing, forgetting, or necessarily even reconciling with the other, because none of these qualities is a moral virtue centered in goodness as is forgiveness. When a person forgives, he does not abandon justice, but instead exercises this virtue along with the mercy that is forgiveness."[45]

Too many times, we struggle with forgiveness because we don't understand what is required of us. We assume letting go would mean condoning or accepting the bad behavior, opening ourselves up to repeated poor treatment. But this is not the case.

My father's repeated offenses, both in neglecting me personally and in his bad behavior in the world, created painful emotions that I needed to learn to deal with, understand, and let go of. But in the process, I could also define an appropriate relationship going forward.

Forgiveness does not require a full embrace, pretending no wrongs have been done. After all, the pardoned Balal was free of the condemnation of death, but not free to return to society. Justice, well-seasoned with mercy, created a future for him and his family without the finality of death, but more importantly, it created freedom for Alinejad in a way that resentfulness could not.

An act of true forgiveness is a way to empower people to move on, even if it is in a more cautious and guarded manner. It is

45   Adam Cohen, "Research on the Science of Forgiveness: An Annotated Bibliography," *Greater Good Magazine*, October 2004. https://greatergood.berkeley.edu/article/item/the_science_of_forgiveness_an_annotated_bibliography.

the clearest embodiment of losing the naiveté of childhood without sacrificing a hope for the future.

CONFRONT THE NEED TO FORGIVE

After a number of years testing boundaries and questioning the path forward, I reached a new point in my journey of forgiveness with my father. I began to wonder if my resentment was preventing him from making needed changes in his life. I wondered if feeling judged by his children and others created such force and shame that he struggled to let go, as though he didn't have the power to change himself. If we model trust and belief for others when theirs is not strong—could forgiveness operate the same way? Could letting go facilitate a miracle, lending him a belief that change is possible when he might not have thought so himself?

The answer was yes—and no.

I'm reminded of an old edition of *Reader's Digest*, first published in 1965, which included a tale of forgiveness after time served. In the story, a man sat on a railroad coach next to a younger man who looked clearly and visibly depressed. After a bit of conversation, he found out the man was a paroled convict returning from a distant prison. The man listened to the story about the shame imprisonment had brought to his family, and how he hadn't received many visits or even letters while incarcerated. The younger man was afraid that this was evidence of unforgiveness, though it could have been a symptom of time or financial constraints.

In his concern, the young man had written one final letter to his family, asking them to put up a signal to him when the train passed by their little farm. If they had forgiven him, they were to put a white ribbon in the big apple tree that stood near the tracks. If they didn't want him to return, they were to do nothing at all, and he would remain on the train as it traveled westward beyond his home.

His apprehension grew as the train drew closer to the farm, and he asked the man next to him for help. He said, "In five minutes, the engineer will sound the whistle, and that will signal the long bend that opens up into the valley where my home is. Will you look for the apple tree on the side of the road? Will you let me know if there is a white ribbon in it?"

When the shrill sound of the train's whistle blew, the young man asked again, "Can you see the tree? Is there a white ribbon in it?"

The man replied, feeling that he had witnessed a miracle, "I see the tree, and I see not one ribbon but many. There must be a white ribbon on every branch. Surely someone does love you." The love and forgiveness extended in that one gesture washed over the man. His outlook on life and himself changed, even his appearance changed, giving him the power to change himself as well.

Sometimes, when we have been hurt, we think the offending party is responsible for taking the first step—that the young man would have to return home and prove something before earning full forgiveness. Perhaps, in a world full of fairness, that would be true to say. But the world isn't a fair place, or we wouldn't have been unduly hurt in the first instance. Who wants fairness anyway? Doesn't that rob us of the chance to be kind? To show compassion, mercy, generosity, selflessness, and forgiveness?

My younger children demand fairness on a daily basis. "He's been on your phone longer than I was. It's my turn. It's not fair." Or, "Why is it my turn to do the dishes? He didn't do it properly yesterday, and I'm carrying his load now. It's not fair." The list is actually quite extensive, from a child's perspective, on the inequalities in the world and how heinously impacted they are by it. It's *unfair* that they have to shower today, or that they have to go to school again when they went yesterday. It's *unfair* that Josh gets to drive his own car to school and Noah doesn't. Nevermind that Josh is seventeen and Noah is seven. It's *unfair* that they have to eat vegetables, go to bed on time, share something or do anything I ask on a regular basis. In fact, you may notice a recurring theme. What we often say is "unfair" is often another word for "it's my reality, but I don't want to do it." If fairness is weighing you down, it might be an interesting exercise to write out a list of what seems unfair and see how much of it is simply uncomfortable, but reality.

What we have instead of fairness is true connection to one another, and forgiveness is the loving tie that binds.

As an adult son, my relationship with my dad is marked with more nuance than in my youth, and it's based firmly in reality since his prison time. It's a stark contrast to the nonconfrontational desire to cover up all wrongs and turn him into a pretense of the picture-perfect dad. In this way, the mask of "forgiveness" that brushes everything under the carpet isn't forgiveness at all, but an escape of the confrontation that is required before we can truly let hurts go and move on.

It took difficult conversations—ones that I struggled to have and that he struggled to hear, but that were necessary to create the closure needed to move on.

And as for the miracle: he never came back to me to apologize. He continued to make mistakes. My forgiveness wasn't meant to control him, but to release my own growth. I had to learn to forgive him anyway. While he had no excuse for his behavior, we had confronted our issues and I had no reason to hold on to them beyond what was necessary to maintain boundaries. I could put ribbons all over our proverbial tree, knowing that I would hope for a similar reception should the roles be reversed. I love him to this day, I'm glad he's my dad, and I wouldn't trade him, even though I don't really trust him.

Forgiveness is a gift given freely, absolutely, and completely, meant to liberate the giver and create the option for liberation in the receiver. Whatever they choose to do with it, we can still remain free.

Like patience, forgiveness does not come from a place of weakness or complacency, but requires courage and moral strength. Without confronting the issues and setting them right wherever possible, they hang about like millstones around our necks, threatening to drown us in our own bitterness and regret. Our conscience will not let us move forward without confrontation and resolution.

Hope College's Charlotte vanOyen-Witvliet and her co-investigators identified physiological effects that came with holding a grudge. The study theorized that forgiveness may free the wounded person from a prison of hurt and vengeful emotions. Indeed, they found forgiveness to yield both emotional and physical benefits, including reduced stress, less negative emotion, fewer cardiovascular problems, and improved immune system performance.[46]

---

46   Adam Cohen, "Research on the Science of Forgiveness: An Annotated Bibliography," *Greater Good Magazine*, October 2004. https://greatergood.berkeley.edu/article/item/the_science_of_forgiveness_an_annotated_bibliography.

Of seventy Hope College undergrads, half were to rehearse forgiving someone who hurt or mistreated them, and the other half were to retain unforgiveness. For the exercise, forgiveness included empathizing with the offender and letting go of negative emotions to be replaced with conciliatory ones. Unforgiveness meant rehearsing the hurt and holding a grudge.

As one remembered the offenses, their psychophysiological responses, emotional responses, and facial expressions all showed a healthier profile in those who forgave compared with those who did not, including a lower arterial blood pressure for the group practicing forgiveness, and some of the changes persisted into the recovery period of the study.

The reactivity they noted compared to a prolonged sense of fear and anger.

Not only is forgiveness active, but unforgiveness is as well. We're either burying our head in the sand and refusing to face our problems, or consciously nursing a grudge to feed the fear and anger we've grown used to accommodating. Real forgiveness requires confrontation—if not with the other person, then with ourselves and our emotions.

While I wish I could get my dad's perspective and hear his apologies, I reached a point where I could identify what a healthy relationship with him was going to look like. It wasn't excusatory or justifying and it wasn't dismissive, but at the same time, it was forgiving and compassionate. In that space, we found a version of a relationship that was very different than my childhood dream, but much more real than those fantasies could ever be. My dad—as his own flawed, vulnerable person—could actually be in that relationship with me, rather than pretending, running, or hiding.

Forgiveness is reaching a point where the past no longer represents fresh and active pain, and we are ready to face the present and walk forward, untethered, into the future.

RELEASE EXPECTATIONS OF THE WORLD

Sometimes our lot in life is just as difficult to let go of as any direct offenses.

As a child, I remember hanging out with a friend who seemed to have all the advantages that life could afford. His parents were strong, intelligent, wealthy, and happily married people. His family was well-respected in our community, and he was a tall, athletic, intelligent kid to boot. Meanwhile, I was this small, late bloomer kid who came from a broken home that wasn't well off and wasn't well respected. I spent years feeling like I didn't have the leg up that someone like him had started with.

Ironically, as my career took off, I struggled as a parent who was now able to give my children the life I wanted to have as a child. In fact, it's a concern I still wrestle with at times. I want them to have the comforts I yearned for and the wisdom I gained but not the suffering that gave it. Such conflict is at the heart of this book. We cannot have both. We cannot give birth to a new self without experiencing the pain of delivery. But what an exciting new world awaits us when we come out the other side.

THE WRONG SIDE OF THE TRACKS

As I have learned to let go of the hang-ups from my past and the labels that I or others put on me, I have discovered that both privilege and the lack of it are equals in life. They don't make us, and they don't break us. What sets us apart and gives us potential is how we choose to respond to what we are given. And the exciting thing is—every day we are given a new chance to respond.

When I was about twenty-eight, an older lady who had only known me for a few years stopped to talk with me. In a kindly moment, she said with praise, "It's wonderful to see you doing so well. Clearly, with who you are and the family you've got, you must have had a wonderful upbringing with proud parents."

In looking at me, she assumed I'd been given every opportunity in life from an early age. She pictured a strong family with strong values, and assumed the life I enjoyed was attributable to those predictable things. But that wasn't really the case.

What I had then was because I confronted what I didn't have before. In fact, I'd privately held on to my childhood situation like a chip on my shoulder until a leader in my church asked me, "Do you see yourself as a child of God with divine potential, or do you see yourself as a kid who grew up on the wrong side of the tracks and just happened to get lucky?"

The question was pointed because he knew that my answer was not going to be the right one. No matter what I achieved, it was never good enough for me because I didn't believe I was good enough, period. I had just happened to get lucky.

Trauma and tragedy shape our paradigms and self-beliefs. It's one thing to let go of the bitterness surrounding those circumstances, but quite another to reshape the beliefs that they formed. Please read those last two sentences again. It took me more than ten years to figure that out! I spent a lot of time and energy trying to forgive others and let go of heartaches and trauma and did so quite successfully. But I found that even when peace replaced pain, I struggled in other ways. It took a long time to learn because I didn't see the connection. I found peace. I forgave. I let go and moved on and consequently didn't suffer. But subconsciously, I still thought less of myself and then acted accordingly. Why? Because in my mind, I was a good guy for being able to move on, but I was still the kid that grew up on the wrong side of the tracks. I just got lucky. That was an incorrect belief that grew out of the difficulties I had strived to let go of. But I was so focused on mending relationships and doing right that I failed to look closely at the beliefs my circumstances created about me. They needed to change also. I had to let go of past beliefs, resentment, and entitlement if I was going to move forward in my life.

RELINQUISH HARSH SELF-JUDGMENT

My wife loves to dance. I, on the other hand, am pathetic at it and consequently fear it. You may think that "pathetic" is a strong word to describe my dancing skills, but if you saw them, you would change your mind quickly, perhaps thinking of something a little stronger that I'm not inclined to put in print.

At an annual European Management Conference many years ago, all spouses or partners of the managers were invited to attend the end of year celebrations in thanks to their supportive efforts. One evening offered music and dancing after dinner. This excited Kim and caused private dread and panic in myself. Even so, I jumped onto the dance floor with her as soon as a large enough crowd had gathered for me to camouflage myself with. I wanted Kim to have a great time and knew I had to just suck this one up and get on with it. (So romantic!)

After a while, however, I started to loosen up a little. I could feel confidence growing and my movements seemed to me to be both rhythmic and dynamic. Then I spotted a floor to ceiling mirror near the other end of the dance floor, and I cleverly shimmied us in that direction to catch a glimpse of the impressive dancing for myself. What I saw was not what I felt. I looked stiff and uncomfortable, tense and ill at ease. My goodness, and this was *after* I had loosened up!

I have wondered many times why I would love to be able to dance and yet simultaneously dread the very thought of it. My wife has explained, "It's not that you *can't* dance, Ben. It's that you *won't*. And you don't because you take yourself too seriously."

She's right. I don't like the idea of looking stupid or making a fool of myself.

In becoming my own harshest critic, I have created self-fulfilling cycles of judgement, seriousness, and mistakes that I can't seem to remedy on the dance floor.

This isn't an easy task. Mahatma Gandhi once said, "Forgiveness is an attribute of the strong." The hardest part of the endeavor to unravel broken beliefs is not so much in the forgiving of others but in forgiving ourselves for our own shortcomings and mistakes—letting go and loosening up as we move through this life.

However the practice manifests, at some point, we have to allow ourselves to be forgiven. We have to stop apologizing for the same thing over and over again. We must be patient with our own failings and mistakes and learn to let go of the shame they create in order to move forward in confidence.

Forgiving ourselves requires a release of both guilt and shame in an extraordinary effort of reformed self-beliefs.

Guilt is a healthy, outward emotion designed to help us improve and correct our wrongdoings. Shame is an inward emotion that holds on to the mistake. Guilt says *what I did was wrong*, while shame says *I am wrong*. In shame, we've let ourselves down, disappointed and maybe hurt other people, and found it difficult to release, even if the other person has expressed forgiveness toward us.

This ongoing fear of the dance floor suggests to me that I have a long way to go with working on this weakness, so let me join you in accepting the challenge to not take ourselves too seriously. Let's let go of the silly things that we bind ourselves with. Let's not get caught up with unnecessary shame or imperfections. We are human and should give ourselves room to be. Let's not be too harsh with ourselves. Kindness is a virtue that must reach inwards to ourselves as well as outwards to others.

"To forgive is to set a prisoner free and discover that the prisoner was you." —Lewis B. Smedes

ESTABLISH A PRACTICE OF FORGIVENESS

As the old story goes, elephant trainers could tie up a baby elephant with a heavy chain around their ankles to keep them in place. Once the chain kept the baby secured, they would then move on to a rope. It wasn't the strength of the rope holding it back, but the strength of the elephant's belief that it couldn't break free.

As the elephant grew, it would continue to assume that the rope would hold him, and wouldn't struggle or fight it. A full-grown elephant would keep itself tied down by a simple rope.

Of course, it's the same for us. We are often held back by little things. Yet each time we strive for forward movement, that little rope pulls on our ankles, keeping us from reaching our full potential. Frustratingly, the things that hold us back can so often be small and easily resolved if we would just be willing to let them go. The surest road downhill is often the gentlest one, so let's be sure to not to ease ourselves into a downward spiral simply because the slow corners are convenient or comfortable. It's time to pull the rope off. Forgive the little things and do it frequently.

> We will enjoy freedom and forgiveness in our own lives when we extend forgiveness to others.

As we let go of "should" statements and other paradigms that we've used to cope with our circumstances and our struggles, it's ultimately the ego that we're releasing. It is a self-protecting inner mechanism that prefers to hold on to resentment as evidence of harm done and dreams missed. Our ego is excellent at justifying feelings of offense and regret.

None of this is truly justified, of course, but it does create a heavy lift for us as we strive to let go. Choosing to not be offended, offering forgiveness when we are wounded, and letting go of hurts and disappointments requires much effort and deliberate sacrifice on our part. Our ego would have us falsely believe that we are strong and in control for holding on, but we are stronger for letting go. Forgiveness is always the more courageous path.

DAILY PRACTICES

Our inner world is affected by forgiveness as much as it is by injustice. When we let go and forgive, we are offering merciful goodness in its place. It is not approval or condoning of the circumstances, but a choice to be merciful and kind.

However, we need to understand that this is a practice that might take commitment and recommitment. We might say something is water under the bridge, only to find it flooding again later on.

Learning to forgive is a practice quite similar to learning to swim. It happens in degrees. As I've helped each of my children learn to swim, I've noticed a pattern of progression. Nervously, they start out clinging on to me or their mum, uncomfortable at the thought of simply getting wet. The whole experience is totally new to them. In time, they learn that getting wet is fun and they start to splash.

As toddlers, this can often mean they splash themselves in the face and give themselves an unexpected shock. Each one grows at their own pace in this journey but eventually they are at ease with getting water splashed in their faces and this enables them to bravely put their head under the water for the first time. With plenty of cheering and encouragement, the action is repeated, and so it goes until fear has left them. In time, the armbands come off, I remain in arm's reach, and eventually, with practice, they are swimming with confidence.

Now that they are older, my task as dad has moved from bouncing them in the water to throwing them as high into the air as possible to the immediate sound of "Again, again!" Then the teenagers hope to throw me to prove their manhood.

So goes the growth of forgiveness. Small, repeated steps grow our confidence, desire, and ability to take bigger steps. The more we swim in the waters of forgiveness, the more we enjoy it, and the more capable we become. On some days, this practice will feel wonderful, and on other days you'll want to pull your hair out.

The effort required to foster a consistent spirit of forgiveness is fueled by a sense of gratitude. Learning to look for lessons, opportunities, growth, and newfound wisdom can help us see the value that this practice offers. Remember that it's not happy people who are thankful, it's thankful people who are happy. Rest assured that as you gratefully let go (which can be hard at times), you put yourself on the path to greater happiness and emotional prosperity. So let's not stand out in the cold and miss out on the adventures that lie in the waters before us. Start off in the shallow end if you must, but it's time to jump in.

A PATH TOWARD LETTING GO

1. Acknowledge that letting go is a choice.
2. Examine the degree to which injustice or hurt has affected our emotions ("How am I feeling right now as a consequence of this situation?").
3. Consider the alternative to an intentional release ("If I don't let go of them, what is going to happen? Where will they go on their own?").
4. Assess the impact of those emotions, especially anger, hatred, and resentment.
5. Name the opposing emotions, such as peace, love, and acceptance.
6. Determine ways you can nurture the positive emotions.

CONSTANT PERSPECTIVE

Sadly, it's easy to take a moral high ground in one moment only to find ourselves falling short the next. Surely then, the teaming evidence of our own imperfections and inadequacies can inform our decisions when it comes to forgiving others. Especially when we need so much of it ourselves.

The final step in the progressive development of our capacity to forgive is empathy and a willingness to offer an abundance of goodness and mercy to the other person. This is where emotional health is restored and forgiveness takes deep root. It is the highest level of forgiveness, not only to let go of hurts but to show abundant kindness in its place. It is learning that we *want* to extend love and charity toward that person, even more than we feel obligated to. It's not a "should" behavior motivated by duty. It's a deep-rooted desire motivated by love.

This state doesn't occur right away. We certainly aren't infants in the paddling pool here. In fact, it's more towards the deep end of the adult pool. For me, it wasn't until many years of work had gone by before I arrived here. But the destination is worth the long road to get there. The waters are warm and inviting, and the depth creates a calm stillness that brings clarity and tranquility.

> It's not happy people who are thankful, it's thankful people who are happy.

The best version of yourself will walk through life feeling open and present to the opportunities around you, connected to great support, and driven toward meaning and purpose. You will begin to see yourself, your circumstances, and others with new eyes. We are all more than our struggles and weaknesses. And unchained and unencumbered by hurts and false beliefs, you will be empowered to run further, jump higher and leap with greater faith and confidence towards a stronger self.

Each of these virtues interweave to create a complete, whole new version of ourselves—a brand new character, developed by degrees, over time, and through patient practice.

Before we can walk the path to betterment, we must pave it ourselves, brick by brick, laying down the heavy weight of the past and moving forward into a new future. It is painful in the moment, but the vision of a possible future empowers each step. Each textured, rough brick that leaves calluses on our hands makes way for a brighter, smoother stone in the path ahead.

CREATE A VISION OF YOURSELF

What does the best version of yourself look like? Take some time to imagine that person, including the virtues we're pursuing: unfettered by resentment; filled with love and forgiveness toward all people; empowered toward kindness and patience in the face of adversity; having control over your emotions and an insatiable hunger to learn more about yourself, your peers, and the world. Now place those virtues into the context of your life. Create a vision of yourself, free of the past, that's worth working toward.

Ask yourself these questions:

- Is there anyone in your life that needs your forgiveness?
- Do you need their apologies in order to forgive?
- What is your relationship with yourself like?
- Are there things you've done wrong that you need to forgive and let go of?
- What are some daily practices you can work on to make forgiving others and yourself a positive way of being?
- How would you feel if you didn't hold any grudges, hold on to any resentments, and had forgiven all offenses?
- Is such a state possible and worth it to you? If so, what are you doing about it?

Chapter 9

VIRTUE #6: DILIGENT WORK

OUR FUTURE STATE REQUIRES MORE OF US THAN WE EXPECT, BUT WE ARE MORE CAPABLE THAN WE KNOW

If we want to get different results and move forward to better places and higher positions in life, then we need more of a differentiator than natural ability alone. After all, even the one in a million has seven thousand others just like him. To conquer our demons, obtain new opportunities, stand out in the crowd, and reach our ultimate potential, there's a lot of work ahead of us.

Take, for example, the work ethic that Picasso displayed. For all of his talent, even as one considered to be a child prodigy, he continued to practice his craft to an impressive degree until the end of his life.

Before his first breakthrough piece of art, he had already produced 7,300 pieces over twenty years. Between the ages of eight and ninety-one, he produced an estimated 50,000 artworks, including 885 paintings, 1,228 sculptures, 2,880 ceramics, 12,000 drawings, and thousands of prints, tapestries, and rugs. That's an approximate 30,295 days spent working on his craft, or more than one new piece of art every single day.[47]

Or, in light of the devastating loss of Kobe Bryant, we can recall the work ethic that made him one of the NBA's best players of all time. Once, with a cast on his wrist, he famously began practice three hours earlier than everyone else to compensate for the injury.

Then there's Tom Brady and his four Super Bowl wins, who followed a strict diet regiment planned out a year in advance. Or Mozart, who was not simply born a great musician, but trained as a concert pianist and composer from the age of four. Elvis Presley sold over 500 million records, more than any other solo artist at the time, and in 1955 performed 315 shows in 365 days. Gary Vaynerchuk, in spite of having a multimillion-dollar business, continues to work eighteen-hour days. Marissa Mayer, the CEO of Yahoo, wrote of her time at Google: "When reporters write about Google, they write about it as if it were inevitable. The actual experience was more like, 'Could you work 130 hours in a week?'"[48]

Time and again, hard work expended over great lengths of time is projected as a path to success—and it is.

An enduring work ethic is required of us, but there is more at play as well. A man named Scott Young said this: "When

---

47 Mayo Oshin, "Pablo Picasso on the Myth of Overnight Success," Thrive Global, February 2019. https://thriveglobal.com/stories/pablo-picasso-myth-overnight-success/.

48 Eugene Kim, "Yahoo CEO Marissa Mayer explains how she worked 130 hours a week and why it matters," Business Insider, August 2016. https://www.businessinsider.com/yahoo-ceo-marissa-mayer-on-130-hour-work-weeks-2016-8.

working toward a goal, everyone takes a look at their inputs and then examines their results. Most people have learned to view the major input as effort." In other words, if I want to become a millionaire, I'll need to put in a certain amount of effort to achieve it. What we give determines what we get.

Yet there are plenty of people on the lower end of the financial spectrum who work just as hard or harder than anyone else—the same input without the guaranteed output.

In response, Young identifies three other facets of work that help us attain a desired future state: creativity, relationships, and learning. He says, "Efforts should take a back seat to the amount of creativity, relationships, or learning we require. If you want to become a millionaire, you'll need a certain amount of creativity, connections, or understanding to get there."[49]

The virtue of work is not a brute force effort to manipulate outcomes. That kind of physical and mental strain is unsustainable, especially when working in isolation. Mozart may have had natural talent, but his father chose to connect him with teachers. NBA and NFL superstars have coaches and nutritionists. Leaders in Silicon Valley were actually in and near Silicon Valley and all of the connections that creates.

As we examine the creativity, connections, and understanding required to make our work rewarding, remember the vision that set you on this path in the first place. For we do not work for its own sake, but rather as the medium that will shape us into the person we're meant to be.

---

49 Thomas Oppong, "Hard Work is Not Enough," Thrive Global, February 2018. https://medium.com/thrive-global/if-all-you-do-in-life-is-work-really-hard-you-are-never-going-to-be-successful-1550f58bf127.

"Vision without work is daydreaming, work without vision is drudgery, but work coupled with vision is destiny."— Thomas S. Monson

WORK WITH A PURPOSE

When I was a young dad, my little boy had a kindergarten sports day that all the parents attended. Typically those days are held in high school, but this one was for little three- and four-year-old children. All the more memorable, it was a dress-up day. With their parents in tow, dozens of cuddly little children dressed as garden gnomes, fairies, and other fantastic creatures bounced along a string of sports events set up by their teachers.

By far, my favorite event was a simple race. All of the parents lined up along the side of a race track, with cameras out and hearts bursting with pride. For the most part, we were there to enjoy how cute our children could be, each of us feeling like ours had won in that category. Meanwhile, at the finish line, a number of teachers stood with bags of sweets to entice the children to run to the end of the race as we cheered them on.

Simple, and yet quite challenging for a small child running high on sugar and his parents' attention.

In the first heat, one little child ran out ahead of the others, crossing the line first as the adorable winner of the race. But when she crossed the finish line, she just kept on running. And all of the other children who crossed the line kept following her. A mad scramble began, as teachers and some of the parents took off after the kids, chasing them and calling out to them that the race had finished.

Then the next round began. Again, one child emerged in the front and the others followed behind—until the little leader's gnome hat blew off of his head and flew away. As he chased after his hat, all the other children followed, and the race took a swooping curve to the right.

In the third go, one mother got particularly enthusiastic in cheering for her child, who was doing the best he could but was decidedly not out in front. She called out competitively, "Hurry, you can do it, you can do it!" But when she screamed out his name, he misunderstood the noise and stopped in the middle of the race, crying and heartbroken that his mother was upset with him. Instead of finishing, he ran over to her seeking comfort and assurance that he was a good boy—while she apologized and assured him that he wasn't in trouble, she also rejected his appeals for cuddles, gently pushing him away and back toward the race.

It was absolute, wonderful chaos.

Yet how many of us are running through life, as fast as we can, desperately hoping to achieve something but we don't know what? We're following the crowd, but they don't know where they're going either. Our attention is pulled to the sidelines and the target is lost. It's not as cute for us as it was for kindergarteners in gnome hats.

If I'm a hard worker but haven't disciplined my heart, educated myself, or learned to exercise patience or let go of the past, work will only take me so far. We've got to have a reason to be in the race. We've got to have a reason to fight when it gets tough. When opportunities come our way, we've got to have a reason to grab them and run with them rather than passing them by.

Recall James Clear's two-step process for great change in chapter 7: decide the person we want to be, and use small wins to prove to ourselves we can reach that objective.

The story of the hero, familiar to us all in the movies we watch and books that we read, begins with a purpose. Daniel Rodic breaks the formula of the hero into three parts: the call to action (purpose), the trials and tribulations (work), and the eventual victory over the challenge (future state).[50] What's not easily conveyed in the medium of film is how difficult and enduring the trials and crises can be. For the sake of the viewer's or reader's attention span, the journey is greatly condensed, but our heroes perform extraordinary amounts of work over prolonged periods of time in order to achieve success.

For the change of heart to be complete—to turn the called into the hero victorious—time is a necessity. We need to do the work, in deep and meaningful ways, in order for us to get the wisdom.

Without working toward our vision for the future, we've done little more than a child wishing on a star. For false hope only sounds appealing to those who have no hope. What we really need is a sense of true hope, a vision of what we can become, and a path to follow to get there.

As we look to the future, hoping for a personal journey of transformation, we must first create a clear vision of what we're striving to become, then hold it in our mind's eye as we strive diligently and strategically toward it.

---

50 Daniel Rodic, "There Is No Secret to Success—There Is Just Hard Work," The Observer, December 2016. https://observer.com/2016/12/there-is-no-secret-to-success-there-is-just-hard-work/.

WORK SMARTER

K. Anders Ericsson, a professor at Florida State University and a world-renowned performance psychologist once issued this warning: "If you don't try hard, no matter how much talent you have, there's always going to be someone else with a similar amount of talent who outworks and outperforms you."[51]

For many of us, this is a hard pill to swallow. For others, it becomes the chip on their shoulder.

There was a season in my life when I attributed my success to my work ethic and little else. My responsibilities took me from one country to the next on a regular basis, traveling three weeks out of four for a seven or eight-year stretch. The long hours returned pay raises, promotions, a track record of success, good experience, and I inevitably got the jobs that I applied for.

On occasion, when I was teaching, I found myself saying, "I might not be the smartest person in the room, but I will outwork everyone."

It was my mantra—and it was little more than false humility coupled with heavy bragging.

As time went on, I realized that outworking everyone is not a formula for success. The more I was asked about ways to replicate my financial and career success, the more I had to analyze what I did to determine what I could actually teach. My "I'll outwork everyone" message was not enough.

---

51 Ibid

What I learned as I reflected on my journey was the paradox of hard work in relation to this empowerment process. I realized that we have to work like everything depends on us, but simultaneously understand and humbly respect that it doesn't. Hard work plays a part, and so too does talent. But timing, location, awareness, relationships, and creativity are essential also. And dare I say it: luck and good fortune also play a part, though relying on luck is not a strategy either. We must give luck its rightful nod when it appears but never depend on it.

As I looked to those enthusiastic entrepreneurs, anxious to make their mark and reach for the skies, I saw the solution of a multifaceted perspective on hard work needed to be taught. Hard work consists of physical, mental, emotional, social, and creative efforts to maximize the return on our investment of time.

Only perfect practice makes perfect.

My stepfather comes to mind, who set a strong example of hard work. Even when he cut the grass, he would set the pace of a jog. He modeled the idea that working harder than everyone else would always secure the job. Growing up, I took that to mean I should always work the most, and make sure that work was seen. I put in the hours, sacrificed, and did the arduous work necessary to get ahead.

The now-famous ten thousand hours of work is held up as a motivating example, but what if those ten thousand hours are spent doing something the wrong way? What will be become masters of then? My music teacher taught me that perfect practice makes perfect. Bad practice entrenches bad habits. So, time invested in learning, working, and building relationships should be time well spent, not simply spent for its own sake.

A great example of this is all the hard work I put into trying to figure out my mind when it was not my friend. This time and effort came pre-diagnosis, and I studied, practiced, and worked like crazy to sort things out in my head. But not knowing what I was dealing with actually saw me entrench bad habits and intensify negative beliefs. While I improved in many areas, I compromised myself in others. When I understood what I was working with, my learning journey changed and my approach to hard work was more balanced. I teamed up with some well-educated support people, and it made a huge difference.

With any degree of success, enduring labor and sacrifice will be required. Yet in our work, we need to be skilled, efficient, self-directed, and well connected. Working smarter allows us to sustain and propel that success into the future.

WORK IN CONNECTION WITH OTHERS

The strongest heroes come with the greatest character development. Each struggle is meant to change them in some small or big way, and without that growth, even the most action-packed story can come off unfulfilling—or worse, turn the hero into the villain. The corrupting effect of power alters self-perception and affects relationships.

Good stories come with turmoil, persisting over a great portion of the story, requiring much of our heroes. And that's where the best heroes are made.

In a study done by the Greater Good Science Center, self-perceived greatness and deservedness were put under the figurative microscope.[52] Three students were left in a lab at a time, and one was randomly assigned to be a group leader as they worked on a particular task. Thirty minutes into the experiment, four chocolate chip cookies were delivered to the center of the table.

In most cases, the assigned leader took the extra cookie and ate it themselves, often noisily so, as if they had deserved it and wanted everyone to know.

In the King James Version of the Old Testament of the Bible, the book of Ecclesiastes says something that researchers, psychologists, philosophers, and economists prove true time and again: "The race is not to the swift, nor the battle to the strong, neither yet bread to the wise, nor yet riches to men of understanding, nor yet favor to men of skill—*but time and chance happeneth to them all.*"

We do need to be fast, strong, wise, and people of skill, but time and chance will come to all of us. In some moments, it will be a fortuitous, random act of luck and good fortune, and in others, it will feel like senseless adversity. When we hold ourselves up above the factors of time and chance and circumstance, we hold ourselves above others as well. We start to treat them with a lower degree of empathy and consideration. Yet effective work rarely happens in isolation.

We've heard the saying, "It's not what you know, it's who you know," but in actuality, it's who knows *you* that matters. Stepping into the right circles—and, more importantly, becoming

52 Jill Suttie, "What Drives Success, Hard Work or Luck?" *Greater Good Magazine*, April 2016. https://greatergood.berkeley.edu/article/item/success_hard_work_luck.

the caliber of person that someone would want to connect with—creates opportunity that we cannot force our way into. When you're the kind of leader who will share the extra cookie, you forge working relationships that will support your efforts and return dividends. Passing the opportunity forward grows our character, while becoming self-absorbed in the belief that our successes came only from ourselves is isolating and leaves us emotionally stunted.

Sometimes the ball is passed to me when someone else neglects an opportunity, or I'm brought along when someone else accepts one of their own. From time to time, I could create that luck for others, hiring people who had the mindset and heart that would appreciate it, run with it, and make something of themselves because of it.

One of my first management jobs came as a result of my boss taking a chance on me, even though I was remarkably under-qualified. He saw not only my work ethic and that I put in the hours, but that I was trainable and always learning a better way of working. That one opportunity paved the way for my career, and I have been able to pass similar opportunities along to others when given the chance.

If I'm of the frame of mind that I have worked hard, that I do have a natural level of ability and skill, but also that I have been blessed with opportunities beyond my natural contribution, it's going to affect the way I interact with others. When we recognize that there are factors beyond our control that contribute to our success, we have a greater sense of gratitude and generosity.

A researcher by the name of Yuezhou Huo conducted a study in which students were broken up into groups of three, and each asked to list one of three things: external factors beyond their control, personal qualities they possessed or actions they took, or for the control group, undirected reasons that explained events that had occurred.[53] Afterward, each were given the opportunity to donate part of their participation fee to a charity.

Those who had listed external reasons for their good fortune were found to give 25 percent more to charities than those who had listed personal qualities, with the control group falling somewhere in between.

A number of factors have combined to place us in the fortunate circumstances that we're in, and that recognition allows us to work with more gratitude.

Interestingly, when I have the most gratitude, I find I also work the hardest. I'm compelled to nurture the relationships around me and to make the most of my opportunities, which then brings about more of the same.

---

53 Jill Suttie, "What Drives Success, Hard Work or Luck?" *Greater Good Magazine*, April 2016. https://greatergood.berkeley.edu/article/item/success_hard_work_luck.

THE VALUE OF A MENTOR

One of the greatest forms of human connection is that of a mentor. I find that informal mentors are just as influential as more formal relationships. I've found many mentors in the form of books, studying the lives of other authors who have life experience that I'd like to learn from. These mentors don't know I exist, but they have coached me through much of life.

Family circles can be another source of informal mentorship. There have also been people in my faith and business circles who have stepped into the role of mentor over time.

Remember, though, that a mentor can't want your success more than you do. Your desired results will not come when you want others to do the lion's share of the lifting.

ACKNOWLEDGE THE ROLE OF LUCK

The hidden rule of working toward an envisioned future is acknowledging that, in spite of our own personal efforts and sacrifices, we're still not in control of everything. This realization doesn't abdicate our responsibilities. Quite the opposite—it fuels them. It helps to motivate a sense of gratitude, humility, and empathy toward others, which only serves to enrich who we are, enrich our relationships, and nurture further opportunities and progress. No semblance of growth is ever achieved in a vacuum or in total independence.

Nassim Nicholas Taleb wrote in *Fooled by Randomness*, "Mild success can be explained by skills and labor. Wild success is attributable to variance."

As outcomes become more and more extreme, the role of luck increases.[54] If Bill Gates, Mark Zuckerberg, or Elon Musk had been born a hundred years ago, would they have still become wildly rich and successful? Perhaps. What if they had been born in a developing country, say Turkmenistan, a hundred years ago, without access to opportunity and technology, just plenty of access to locally consumed wheat. What would their life outcomes look like in that situation?

In their current circumstances, each have massive quantities of natural ability, skill, and strength, but external factors have shaped them as well.

An economist by the name of Robert H. Frank from Cornell University wrote a book called *Success and Luck*, all about the factors of success and roles of luck and hard work. If we consider someone who was born into a good family, in the right neighborhood, in the right time, we'd have high expectations of them to be able to excel in their chosen craft. Not just because of who they are, but also because of the good fortune they enjoy in being able to attend the right schools and receive the right teachers.

Fortunately, luck can be influenced by bending the law of averages to our good with a developed character. If we consistently build relationships with the right people, take responsibility for our own self-directed learning, consistently work hard and

---

54 Michael Shermer, "Does Success Come Mostly from Talent, Hard Work—or Luck?" *Scientific American*, November 2017. https://www.scientificamerican.com/article/does-success-come-mostly-from-talent-hard-work-mdash-or-luck/.

sacrifice, opportunities will arise more than before, and we'll be ready for them when they do. Done well, we can overcome any obstacle and create a life for ourselves that we would be proud of, even if it's different than what we expected to begin with.

Luck is being prepared when opportunity presents itself.

The role of luck doesn't justify quitting or slacking off. As I learned from my childhood jealousies, it is only part of the story. Indeed, good fortune itself might become the struggle required for some to grow into the people they're meant to be. The true measure of a person is not what we get, but what we become. It is how we develop our hearts and minds and actions as a consequence of what life throws our way.

Where I thought I'd be at age twenty is very different from the vision I have for my life at forty. The more developed we become, the more clearly we can see what we can still yet become, which in turn motivates and empowers our choices. As character strengthens, our expectations of life evolve as well. When it does, we can remain flexible with our vision to accommodate where we have control and let go of where we do not. This is why we must pursue a collection of underlying virtues rather than a formula of dos and don'ts.

With time and chance happening to us all, we deserve neither our deepest heartaches nor our greatest privileges. What we do deserve is our greatest commitment and noblest response to whatever life throws at us, be it good or bad.

WHEN WE CAN GO NO FURTHER

I once lived in a neighborhood about two kilometers from a lake that was six kilometers in circumference. When I mentioned to my friend Taff that I was thinking about going for a run around the lake, he laughed and reminded me to do the math. There was no way I could do a ten-kilometer round trip in one go. I had never done it before.

Of course, that was the right thing to say to challenge my ego, so I promised to prove him wrong. I enthusiastically hung up the phone, went to change into some semblance of running gear, and get it done.

By the time I arrived at the lake, two kilometers into the run, I was already wondering what I'd gotten myself into. If I hadn't just spoken to my friend, I probably would have turned around and enjoyed a nice four kilometers and called it a day. But my pride was involved, and there was no way I could prove him right so quickly. I could already tell in my legs and lungs that this was going to be a one-time effort. I was never going to set out on this run again.

So I crossed the street and entered the path that encircled the lake.

The farther I got, the worse I felt. I really hadn't been ready for such a long run—though Taff didn't need to know that. As my pride gave way to exhaustion, ready to give up and head back, I had hit the halfway mark. My internal battle to turn around and go back could end. The only way out was now through.

I had no wallet and no phone with me that would let me catch a bus or call a ride. I kept running, bemoaning the pain in my legs, joints, and lungs while hoping that someone driving by might know me, take pity and give me a lift. Wish as I might, no one passed by. With no one to rescue me and now only a few kilometers left, I finally surrendered to reality.

Funnily enough, once I acknowledged that all I could do was run back home, the experience became easier. I relaxed and began to focus on my pacing and breathing, trying to regulate my energy to make it all the way back. The negative energy spent on unnecessary exit strategies got redirected into completing the task.

Within the hour from the time I left the house, I was home, having finished a 10k run. At the halfway mark, I felt like I couldn't go on. Now I was finished and I could see I was able to do so much more. Necessity helped me see that I was more capable than I felt.

Naiveté made me set a lofty goal. Experience taught me that it was harder than I thought it would be. And when I finally embraced the struggle, I was able to work harder and achieve more than I thought possible.

This is true of any journey, self-inflicted or not. Suffering makes us impatient, with our natural desire being to fight it or flee from it. When we surrender to the elements of suffering that we cannot control, our focus can shift to the opportunities around us to become more, and to find happiness, fulfillment, and meaning. We don't get to choose the duration of the work or the nature of our circumstances, but we can choose our response.

We can often go twice the distance, or more than we think we can go. No matter how far you think you can go, you can keep going. When we're ready to throw in the towel, we can always push a little bit harder. This applies to enduring hardship, learning and developing a new skill, and continuing to work for a future that's yet unseen.

I've begun to ask myself in those moments, "If I just hang in there one more day, one more week, what's going to happen?" Time and again, I'm reminded that the arrow of time continues on at the same pace, regardless of how I feel about it. If we keep on working toward that future state, being patient with ourselves as time moves through us, we can both survive as well as become something better and stronger on the other side. We can begin to thrive.

UPDATE YOUR FUTURE

As you look to the future and envision a more polished and improved you, ask yourself these questions:

- Recognizing the multifaceted nature of work—physical, mental, emotional, social, and creative—what areas need improvement or help?
- What are some external factors that have influenced my life to date?
- How do I feel about them? Am I grateful, resentful, nonchalant? How should I feel about them?
- Are my current efforts aligned with my overall vision for the future? If so, how? If not, why?
- Would the role of a coach or mentor make a difference?
- What parts of my present reality are difficult but need to be accepted?
- How does accepting the difficult give room for new growth?

Chapter 10

VIRTUE #7: WILLFUL SURRENDER

WHEN WE STOP TRYING TO CONTROL *EVERYTHING*, WE GAIN MORE CONTROL OF THE *RIGHT THINGS*

At this stage in my career, I spend a fair amount of time consulting and coaching companies and people on the process of corporate and personal transformation. I regularly speak to audiences about what the journey involves, managing expectations, subduing fears, offering hope and solutions, and providing case studies and research that gives their personal experiences context, perspective, and new insights.

In a strategy meeting recently, I listened as business leaders tossed ideas back and forth regarding their current state of affairs in a particular market. It wasn't insurmountable by any means. Just another storm to weather, as we all must.

After some time, I noticed that they hadn't actually gotten to the bottom of the issue. Before we could overcome anything, we had to acknowledge the problem directly, and that hadn't happened yet.

I paused the meeting and explained that change requires a full understanding of the present moment and what brought us here. We couldn't strengthen their presence in that market without addressing what had weakened it in the first place. In simple terms, mapping transformation is like using GPS in your car: both a starting point and a destination are required to create the ideal route, and it takes time and plenty of maneuvers to get there. If we refuse to type in where we really are, we'll never be able to get where we're going.

In this situation, they needed to know where they were starting as well as how they had gotten there to begin with. So I asked them what the real problem might be, hoping to move the conversation in a more productive direction. Great discussion ensued, but people were nervous to say what the real problems were. Frustratingly, the strength to confront our present realities doesn't appear in a moment, even when we are confronted directly ourselves. Arriving at that point is also a part of the transformative process and these vital virtues certainly aid us in getting there.

As pockets of people stood around chatting after the meeting, a senior executive wisely observed, "Your question created a lot of discussion, but we didn't actually answer the question." Then he thought for a moment and added, "I guess, if we were to answer it truthfully, it could take some of us to quite a dark place."

He was right, and follow up discussions certainly needed to happen to help the right people get there. My response to him was the dark is not a bad starting point. When starting points are pain points—great! Embrace them. Confront them. When we face our pain points directly, transformation can begin. If we can't face them, we'll fail. After all, fertilizer and rain grow more trees than dry ground and clear skies. And we all get our fair share of dirt and fertilizer thrown at us in life.

There is power in a seed being dropped into the dirt, covered in darkness, manure, and rain. Something good happens because of that. But sometimes it feels, while we are lying dormant in the dark, that perhaps nothing will ever come of it. In order to absorb the nutrients of the soil and allow seasons of growth to manifest, the seed must surrender its outer shell. In our case, we must let the ego go.

Even when a tree has grown up tall and strong, there are seasons of barrenness when the leaves must fall and the branches get trimmed back. But it's always followed by a new season, new life, and new growth.

Unfortunately, when we cannot admit the reality of our struggles, we prioritize that tough outer shell of ego and appearances over the opportunity for new growth. Sometimes we keep marching confidently ahead while still tucked into that shell, expending great effort to ignore our true reality. Then we wonder why we're going around in circles instead of reaching our goals.

Removing the reality of our present moment only disempowers us to change it. While it might feel easier to distract from present pain, it is still just a distraction. We might repeat what worked in the past or devote energy to wishful thinking—all of which can feel as though we're employing solutions. But it's superficial discussion without any answers. It's being buried without anchoring our roots for growth.

Even when it feels like we have faced nothing but a perpetual, miserable winter, we can still choose a noble and strong response. We can face present realities with heads held high and shoulders squared, empowered by the paradox that the struggle is part of our joy, and that we must lose a sense of control of our lives in order to more fully gain it. And trust me. Owning your pain points can certainly leave you feeling like you have less control. That's often why we hide from it.

> "When ego is lost, limit is lost. You become infinite, kind and beautiful."—Yogi Bhajan

THE NATURE OF SURRENDER

In the previous chapters, we've seen just how important it is to take full responsibility for our lives, adapting to and drawing strength from our circumstances. We've seen that time and chance happen to all of us, leaving us without total control of what may be happening in our lives. All the while, we remain empowered to respond well and exercise the control we do have. In light of our limited control, our lives demand the constant emotional work of surrender, relinquishing our fight against what cannot be won and simultaneously maximizing control of what can be.

Surrender does not mean giving up—in fact, it's quite the opposite. Similar to letting go of the past, surrender to the present is a confrontational activity that demands more of us than perhaps anything else. At the same time, when we choose to surrender to our present reality, it is a virtue of peace and freedom.

Within chronic struggle and a persistent challenge, struggling to gain control of external factors can be exhausting, especially if it is a fight against the truth of our reality. Surrender is an active choice to let go of the ego-driven need for control, allowing us to change our underlying beliefs about ourselves, our circumstances, and ultimately, our future.

> When starting points are pain points—great! Embrace them. Confront them. When we face our pain points, transformation can begin. If we can't face them, we'll fail.

THE EGO AND A DISTORTED VIEW OF SELF

From a psychoanalytical perspective, ego is the part of the mind that mediates between the conscious and unconscious, responsible for testing reality and creating personal identity. Freud has many layers of definitions of ego, of course, and then there is the sense of self-esteem or self-importance that we often associate with the word.

When I speak of ego, however, it is from a much simpler place. The ego that threatens our ability to surrender is an unhealthy form of self-protection. If someone is egotistical, they're driven by a superiority complex and a sense of self-importance. To let that go is to adjust the distorted sense of identity that drives our own interests above others. It is to let go of the false interpretation that we are more important than we are, more right than we are, more entitled than we are, or that our feelings and agenda are more important than reality.

Ego skews the facts to fit its own interpretation. Surrender is a willingness to adjust, to accommodate truth, and reflect reality. It demands humility. The ego is a broken tool. Refusing to face the dark corners of our lives is valuing our own present self-interest over future possibilities. This behavior does not protect or improve us at all. The only way to reach a better future is to align with reality, relinquishing our stubborn and selfish ego and putting truth front and center, no matter how painful it is. If we deny ourselves the true nature of the present, we deny ourselves the growth it can create in the future.

While some expressions of ego make us bigger than we are, others diminish us, convincing us that we deserve nothing or are less than who we really are. In some of the darkest days of depression I have experienced, a distorted sense of self convinced me that my emotional numbness was the safest choice I could hold to. I embraced my vulnerability too much without acknowledging any of my strengths. I distorted and diminished my perception of self and reality in ways that minimized it and thus minimized my control of it. In this way, ego is tied to the imposter as much as it is to arrogance.

Both extremes are dangerous in what they produce, and both are equally unrealistic in their expression.

The real self exists comfortably in a state of being both nothing and everything. It balances the incredible miracle of who we are, with the flaws, imperfections, and limited control that we possess. When either of those sides become distorted, we have chosen the comfort of ego over the challenge of surrender.

Surrender is an active choice to let go of the ego-driven need for control, allowing us to change our underlying beliefs about ourselves, our circumstances, and ultimately, our future.

SUNK COST AND A DISTORTED VIEW OF THE PRESENT

I once watched my stepdad grimace as he sat down at the kitchen table with the most foul-smelling fish pie I've ever come across in my life. Every bite that he took looked painful. I asked him what he was doing, and he cringed as he replied, "I bought it and don't want it to go to waste." Even worse, it had been on sale for about fifty cents.

How often do we feel obligated to get value out of what we've sunk time and money into, long after the value is gone? Far beyond fish pie, we do this in our beliefs, our personal investments, and our projects. Companies pour thousands of dollars, sometimes millions, into projects that have failed, and will keep investing in them for thousands more, all for fear of losing what has already been spent.

Behavioral economists refer to this as *sunk cost fallacy*.[55] When people continue with a behavior or plan beyond its value to them, it's typically because of previously invested time, money, or effort.

Christopher Olivola, an assistant professor of marketing at Carnegie Mellon Tepper School of Business, conducted a series of experiments constructed to measure the extent to which sunk cost could sway people into making hypothetical decisions.[56] He said this: "Nearly all across the board, the results affirmed the existence and strength of the phenomenon, both as it applies to individuals and to others."

---

55 Jamie Ducharme, "The Sunk Cost Fallacy is Ruining Your Decisions. Here's How." *Time* magazine, July 2018. https://time.com/5347133/sunk-cost-fallacy-decisions/.

56 Ibid.

In one scenario, people were asked to imagine if they were accidentally scheduled to take two trips: one to Montreal and one to Cancun during the same weekend, forcing them to choose one. When they were told that one flight cost $200 and the other $800, people were significantly more likely to opt for the pricier trip, even if they would have preferred the cheaper destination.

In another experiment, participants were asked to imagine that they felt full after eating a few bites of rich cake at a potluck party. Some were told that the cake had been purchased on sale at a local bakery, while others were told the cake was expensive and had come from a shop almost an hour away. Some were told to imagine that they had purchased the cake, and some were told that someone else brought it. Then all were asked whether they would finish the cake despite feeling full. Regardless of who had "bought" the imaginary cake, participants were far more likely to say they'd keep eating the expensive cake compared to the cheaper one, even if they were full.

We have an inbuilt mechanism within us that tries to get the maximum value out of things, and another to avoid loss whenever possible. When those mechanisms are at war, we're left with the sunk cost fallacy. We're doing what we can to avoid loss of what has already been invested, even when it creates more loss than surrender and redirection might.

We persist even when it ceases to return benefits, simply because of what it meant to us in the past. And the cost doesn't have to be great for this to be true, either. Yet when we cling unhealthily to the past, we're likely to miss present opportunities and future possibilities.

On a deeper level, the fear may simply be of acknowledging

their earlier missteps. We refuse to confront the problems in our relationships that have died long ago, unloved and unhappy, but afraid of the alternative. We harbor secret challenges and internal conflicts that we battle day after day—low self-esteem, quiet depression, addiction, heartaches, heartbreak, disappointment, uncertainties, and wounds that refuse to heal—yet say "I'm fine" over and over again, continuing along the same path we've followed for years.

The more we invest in something emotionally, the harder it is to abandon it. Once we've put our heart and soul into something, we don't want to admit when it's time to move on. We want to save face—to believe that it's going to work, not because of where it's taking us but because of what we've put into it.

This, at its core, is ego. It's a distorted view of reality that tells us doing what we've done will get us something other than what we've already gotten.

In its place, surrender asks us to admit that we don't have all the answers and that we are going to need help.

If a market fluctuates, a regulation changes, or a disruption arises, a business that does not adapt will not make it much further. The same applies to us in life. Life changes and takes us along paths that we cannot plan for. Surrendering to present reality allows us to save time, energy, effort, resources, heart, soul, and identity—paradoxically, through the act of losing it.

Surrender isn't giving up on the future, but letting go of our illusions.

THE PRACTICE OF SURRENDER

How can we drive toward achievement while surrendering to contentment in present circumstances? That feels like a contradiction, doesn't it? But it's not. It is a paradox in the same way that we must break muscles down in order to build them up, or to swing a golf club downward in order to hit a ball up in the air, or to step away from the hoop to rebound a basketball.

It is a paradox in the vein of the biblical teaching—lose your life to find it, take the yoke when you feel weighted down. It is the child who is nothing in terms of capability or strength, but everything to her parents.

As we build up the muscles of these virtues, their own apparent paradoxes emerge. Urgency couples with patience, a pursuit of the known supports our faith in the unknown, and a strong sense of desire colors our efforts to release, surrender, and work for our past, present, and future moments, respectively. If our vision is worth pursuing, these virtues interact with much less friction than it seems they would.

When we know what purpose we're driving toward, then it becomes natural for us to let go of some things and grab on to others. To nurture some qualities and temper others. The great balancing act, then, requires identifying a clear vision and keeping it in our sights even as it changes over time.

Viktor Frankl compares the journey of success to the emotion of happiness:

> "Don't aim at success. The more you make it a target, the more you're going to miss it. For success, like happiness, cannot be pursued. It must ensue. It only does so as an unintended side

effect of one's dedication to a cause greater than oneself, or is the byproduct of one's surrender to a person other than oneself. Happiness must *happen*, and the same holds for success. You have to let it happen."[57]

Surrender brings us closer to our desires, often because it asks us to relinquish what has held our attention in place of the steps we must take toward our vision. The white-knuckled grip that we keep on our problems sends them spiraling out of control, even though we desperately want the opposite.

Surrender isn't giving up on the future, but letting go of our illusions. Radical acceptance of the present, including all of its struggles, is the only way to find a path forward out of our pain points. This is a surrender of our need to control everything, precisely so we can focus control on ourselves.

Acknowledging our own mistakes and imperfections is an act of surrendering the ego. Forgiveness and apologies surrender the past. And contentment surrenders comparison in favor of service, humility, and gratitude.

COMPARISON: THIEF OF JOY AND ENEMY OF SURRENDER

Astronomers have long proposed that the naked human eye can see about five thousand stars in the dark, and about a hundred from a brightly lit street. But with the amplification of telescopes, Australian astronomers measured the brightness of all galaxies in one sector of the cosmos, then calculated how many stars that space must contain. At a gathering of the

---

57 Viktor Frankl, *Man's Search for Meaning*, Originally published 1946, Beacon Press edition 2006.

International Astronomical Union conference in Sydney, they presented the number: seventy-six trillion, or a seven followed by twenty-two zeros.[58]

For context, that's more stars in space than the number of grains of sand in all of Earth's beaches and deserts combined. And that's just what's visible within the range of our current telescopes.

If we then take that unfathomable number and acknowledge that many of them will have planets just as our sun does, the size of the universe becomes completely incomprehensible.

Now, amongst the infinite amount of time and space that exists among near numberless scores of stars, and consider that we are each one speck of life on one of those many planets. It's humbling, isn't it? Comparison would put us in the context of the stars—or our colleagues, our neighbors, or the leaders in our fields—and say that we're less than.

Yet, we are quite something, aren't we?

Before my son was diagnosed with nephrotic syndrome, I never once thought about his kidneys, or mine. Yet there they were, cleansing my body on a consistent basis. When was the last time that you were consciously grateful for your kidneys, without a sudden failure to call your attention to it? Or your liver or spleen or pancreas? Often, without the wake-up call of a sudden illness or the constant presence of something chronic, we take our bodies for granted, instead of respecting the living miracles that they are.

58 Andrew Craig, "Astronomers count the stars," BBC News, July 2003. http://news.bbc. co.uk/2/hi/science/nature/3085885.stm.

For every new model of a camera that comes out, we have our own self-correcting lenses with an automatic focus found in our eyes. For every new car that we're so proud to purchase, they still get scratched and dented, while our skin and our bones self-heal under nearly any circumstance. We are simply incredible.

Life is in your beating heart, against all of the millions-to-one odds that you could come into being at the end of a long line of millions-to-one odds that your ancestry came into being. Even if we have nothing but the love of people close to us, we are miraculous, and a culmination of countless miracles.

Comparison would have us focus only on our flaws—the nothingness in the paradox of mankind without the hope and optimism of the other side. Our everythingness. Yet true change can only come to us when we accept the paradox that we are nothing and everything at once, just as joy and suffering are two sides of the same reality.

Let's see ourselves and others all as delicious confections of pure potential, delicately wrapped in imperfection and vulnerability. Then calmly watch comparison and insecurities melt away.

We will become liberated to reach new heights, and we will help others to do the same. We could then humbly let go of our excessive need for control and feel greater peace of mind. We would learn to surrender our illusions with courage and become empowered to shape our reality into something far brighter. A more peaceful now and the thrill of a brighter future ahead is certainly something to be thankful for.

Gratitude becomes fuel for our transformation, vision accelerates it, and good character carries it through to realization, ensuring bumps in the road don't halt our progress.

THE UNNECESSARY FEAR OF LOSS

There is nothing my younger children love more than jumping into my bed to have cuddles while we watch their favorite cartoons. All of them need to rest their head on my arms, which I stretch out wide while they snuggle in close. Even our dog gets in on the action and finds her rightful place curled up on my legs. I think this is one of the most rewarding moments of my day, and I'm pleased to say, it happens a lot.

If there is any victory in life that I've been able to claim, it is that my relationship with my children is my greatest success. I love those kids more than any human expression could possibly convey.

Ironically, in spite of the strong foundations, great relationships, fond memories, fun times, support, sacrifice, and overwhelming love shared, my greatest fear is ending up with broken relationships with my children like my dad has with his. The thought scares me to this day. It is certainly unnecessary, but it definitely fueled my efforts in the past. Past experience for me has created an unfounded fear of loss.

In Daniel Kahneman's book *Thinking, Fast and Slow*, he explains that all decisions involve uncertainty about the future, and in response, the human brain has evolved an automatic and unconscious system to protect against potential loss. Our default setting becomes a focus on the loss rather than potential future gains. Of our naturally inclined perspectives, he writes:

"Organisms have placed more urgency on avoiding threats than they did on maximizing opportunities, and these are more likely to be passed on in our genes. Over time, the prospect of loss has become a more powerful motivator to our behavior than the promise of gain. Wherever possible, we try to avoid losses of any kind, and when comparing losses to gains, we don't treat them equally."[59]

So, let's take a moment to balance the scales. We face both threat and opportunity all the time. But past threats don't need to cloud our present opportunities.

JOY IN THE ACT OF SURRENDER

Viktor Frankl once said that the central theme of existentialism is "to live is to suffer, and to survive is to find meaning in the suffering." I would add to that, that to thrive is to find joy in the meaning. In living, we suffer. In survival, we find meaning. In the discovery of meaning, we thrive.

The level of surrender that growth requires takes great courage.

Suffering exists. There will be mistakes, pain, and adversity lurking when we turn to face our pain points. But we are miracles of creation, destined to step forward in faith, unshackled by the past and firm in our vision of the future. We are given resources of discipline and intellect, immersed in love and tempered by patience. We are an interconnected garden marked by time and chance, nurtured by suffering and weathered in adversity. In our individual weaknesses, we are collectively strong. In our personal imperfections, we are unitedly complete.

---

59 Daniel Kahneman, *Thinking, Fast and Slow*, Farrar, Straus and Giroux, 2011.

We are paradoxes of joy and adversity, and that is the most empowering truth of all.

THE MIRACULOUS SELF

For the purposes of this book, look inward one final time—be honest about who you are, with all of your strengths and weaknesses on display. Then admire them. You are miraculous, in fantastic circumstances. And there is so much more joy for you to know and share.

Ask yourself the following questions:

- What are some illusions that I hold on to?
- How can I let them go?
- How will letting go of pretense and confronting my pain points give me greater strength?
- If this makes me feel vulnerable—how will I manage that and still take action?
- What are some examples of achievements, big or small, that I have experienced that can encourage me to move forward?
- Who can I turn to for extra strength if I need it?
- Is there someone I can support in this process?

CONCLUSION

A HIDDEN TRUTH WITH VISIBLE STRENGTH

The largest living organism on earth rests within Utah's Fishlake National Forest. It covers 106 acres and weighs nearly six-thousand metric tons, and the untrained eye might miss it entirely. It is the Pando colony, which is a forest of genetically identical trees—over forty-thousand trunks—all sharing a single root system. Tree rings indicate that each stem lives for 130 years, on average, and the entire system is believed to be more than eighty-thousand years old.

An entire forest, made up of a single tree, grew to become the largest and oldest living thing on the planet, because of the strength of its interconnected roots.

Imagine the comfort a sapling would have, knowing that the roots and protection of thousands will provide for it as it grows through precarious early years. Imagine a stem on the outskirts of the forest, expanding its borders while being rooted in eighty-thousand years of precedent.

I wonder how we could grow as human beings if we better understood our interconnected roots.

How powerful would we be if one stem of humanity could feel the strength of seven billion others all nurturing and supporting it? How would our vision expand if we felt like an integrated part of the biggest living thing on the planet? What wisdom would we gain if we understood our history not just as our own experiences, but roots going back many millennia?

The Pando colony is a paradox in itself, both old and new at the same time. So too, are we as new stems rooted in deep human history. We only see as far as we can in our generation because we stand on the shoulders of giants. Each one of us are connected to thousands of others by invisible threads that bind us, and those to thousands more.

Any attempt to live for ourselves risks severing our roots from the life force of human connection.

Our individual strength is nothing compared to the power we have in humility, service, and shared empowerment, which is why each of the virtues carries within it a way to relate to those around us.

Applying these principles in isolation can only provide a limited benefit, for it's only when we share with one another in humility—not superiority—that we are fully transformed, reintegrated into the network of virtue and strength that humanity was meant to be.

"He's struck by the notion that he's not just a wave—he's the whole, big, wide ocean." —Jim Carrey, *How Roland Rolls*

EMBRACE THE PARADOX

Even now, after hours spent analyzing the benefits of adversity with me, if I could offer you a stress-free life, human nature would prompt you to take it. I'd be in the same boat. We are more stressed now than ever before, and weary because of it. And we are hardwired to run from it. We still internalize struggle as failure, still hope to control what isn't ours to control, and still wish for reprieve without the required hard work.

In yet another paradox, however, this particular stress comes not from circumstances we don't want, but from our effort to eliminate the negative versus manage it. The more we try to eliminate stress or anxiety, the more we feed it. But we need both the well of suffering and the waters of joy in order to thrive.

As a result of winter, we appreciate spring. As a result of illness, we appreciate health. As a result of death, we appreciate life. The opposing sides are not at war, but so tightly joined that they are sides of the same coin. We cannot have one without the other.

The embrace of suffering empowers us, while resistance robs us of strength.

We're given advantages for growth through our disadvantages in life. We're given joy when we cease to pursue it. We're shaped by our response to the circumstances given to us, but not defined by the struggle itself. To that end, we can and must accept the role that suffering plays in our lives, while keeping our eyes fixed on the discovery of meaning and the joy of purpose.

ENDURE SEASONS WELL

Growth is typically slow. It's an unfortunate fact of life on this planet. At times, when the branches are bare and the air is cold, it can seem like nothing is happening at all. But it's the quiet growth, balancing loss and gain, that builds the strength to endure almost anything.

Almost—but not quite everything. Tragically, the Pando colony is dying.

In the early 1900s, humans aggressively hunted animals such as bears, wolves, and mountain lions that fed on grazing animals in the region. With a decrease in apex predators, the number of grazing animals has grown, and in turn, they are destroying the young growth of the forest.

It's interesting, isn't it? The lack of an aggressive predatorial animal can impact the growth of a forest. As in nature, so in life: the lack of struggle and adversity can bring about a deadening effect that compromises growth and future life.

We need the predators and the grazers, the heat and the winter—with balance being the ultimate objective. When we become heavily tilted toward enduring hardship or preoccupied with an imagined stress-free existence, the ecosystem of personal growth is disrupted. Absent struggle, the forest begins to die.

Balance is not a state of arrival, but a constant striving. An active process by which we shift and move, give and take, to bring excess under control and increase what is neglected. Perhaps, then, the paradoxes exit precisely because we need them to counter each other. We need the friction to create energy for change.

Whether you're a seed that simply feels buried, a sapling hoping to weather the storms, or a big tree with little roots, we all have growth ahead of us. We all have paradoxes to hold and balance to achieve. But on the other side of barren seasons, cleansing fires, and slow, quiet growth lies the harvest of empowerment. The fruit of a higher version of ourselves—a person of vision and faith, who is ever patient, disciplined and always seeking to learn. A person who governs their thoughts and emotions and, as a consequence, themselves.

Transformed by these virtues, rooted in the lessons of adversity, and thriving in the joy of patience and humility, everything about us is changed. We behave better, think better, have better desires, and hold better control over our emotions. We serve better and love better, and as part of humanity's vast network of roots and stems, such goodness can't help but flow back into our lives.

Lifting others serves to lift us as well. Teaching others educates us all the more. Tending to the wounds of others sees our own brokenness healed. And a life devoted to such service nurtures the greater organism, sending our roots out far and wide—well-nourished, strong, and part of the greatest living miracle on earth.

Together, we become anchored against even the strongest storms of life. Together, we become empowered beyond imagining. Together, we can believe more, dream more, hope more, love more, and become more—and it begins with *you*.

You are stronger than you now realize.

You are equipped with more resources and power than you can imagine.

You are a paradox of this beautiful universe, and *you* are not just a stem in the forest.

You *are* the forest.

EPILOGUE

THIRTY DAYS OF PARADOXES TO PONDER

1. The more you try to impress people, the less impressed they will be.
2. As Socrates said, "I am wise only in the sense that I know that I am not."
3. The more you love yourself, the less others love you—but you also need to love yourself so that others can.
4. The more you fail, the more you can succeed.
5. The harder you try, the easier it gets.
6. The more choices you have, the less satisfied you are by them.
7. We often need to fight for peace.
8. The one constant in life is change.
9. Time heals all wounds. It also wounds all heels (okay, that's more of a play on words!).
10. We are both nothing and everything at the same time.
11. You earn love by giving it away.
12. The less we pursue happiness, the greater the chance we have of finding it.
13. The more we chase success, the more it evades us.
14. The more we suffer, the more joy we can experience.

15. The greatest leaders are the greatest servants.
16. Lifting others lightens our own load.
17. Teaching is a form of learning.
18. The more we need others, the less they are attracted to us.
19. Acknowledging weakness is a form of strength.
20. We need to pursue progress and simultaneously be content with where we are in order to be happy.
21. We need to work with urgency and simultaneously be patient with the process in order to achieve excellence.
22. We need to believe more in ourselves and simultaneously recognize our own nothingness in order to become more.
23. We need to have a clear vision of the future and simultaneously acknowledge that we don't truly know it in order to have faith in it.
24. We need to work like everything depends on us and simultaneously understand that in fact, it doesn't in order to maximize our outcomes.
25. Everyone is a combination of strengths and weaknesses at the same time.
26. Statistically, you can literally be one in a million and at the same time have seven thousand other people who are just like you.
27. We are all unique individuals and simultaneously all interconnected.
28. Trying to eliminate stress only creates more of it.
29. We experience poor health and better appreciate good health as a result. The same goes for life and death.
30. We can't be humble and acknowledge it at the same time.

ACKNOWLEDGMENTS

There are many people that have played essential roles in this book. People to whom I am grateful to extend my heartfelt thanks publicly here. This would not have come about without them and it wouldn't have been such an enjoyable experience were it not for their support and contributions.

Firstly, I wish to thank my wife Kim. You sacrificed countless hours of your own precious time so that I could research, write, and publish this work. Your selflessness has been a generous gift to me. I am so thankful to you. Thank you for reading manuscripts and giving candid feedback. Our children likewise have been a wonderful source of encouragement as they have shown boundless confidence and excitement at the potential of this book. You have all buoyed me on with your belief in me.

Thank you to Leah Notarianni and Bucky O'Neill for their initial encouragement for me to get my message out. If not for that push, this book would be still somewhere within me, obscure and unwritten. Also, a big thank you to Leah for introducing me to JT McCormick. I believe that small acts of selfless service can change trajectories with significance. This was such a moment for me. Thank you.

JT, thank you for respecting my story and believing that people need to hear it. Importantly, thank you for agreeing to publish this book as a result. Your entire team at Scribe have been fantastic and professional. I have enjoyed every interaction at every point of the journey.

Thank you to all who have modeled the virtues of the Empowerment Paradox in my career, your leadership has been inspirational—Peter Strydom, Mark Beiderwieden, Frank VanderSloot, Larry Bodhaine and Richard Winwood. I have been graced to be associated and am better because of it. Your examples have added value to *The Empowerment Paradox.*

To all my friends and colleagues at Nikken. I have to fight the strong desire to start mentioning you by name. There are simply too many people to mention personally and I wouldn't like to miss anyone out. Hopefully you see the mission of helping others become more expressed within the pages of this book. Thank you to each of you for your belief and encouragement, support, and devotion.

To Caron Kelly, who worked with me when my personal suffering was at its limits and literally saved me. Thank you. This book is in large part, the embodiment of lessons from the journey you helped me on. A journey that is far from over. For Chris Berry who gave my struggles perspective which have, in turn, flavored this book. To Andy Butterworth for being a personal example of what *The Empowerment Paradox* is all about—thank you.

To all who read and reread sample scripts, gave feedback, edited, worked and reworked the manuscript to help create a polished and finished work. Your contributions are so appreciated.

I cannot even begin to express my gratitude and thanks for Brannan Sirratt. You were my greatest partner in writing this book. Your professionalism, love of the material, belief, enthusiasm, experience, talent, and skill have made this project a pleasure beyond words.

Finally, to adversity. Thank you, my old friend, for being my greatest teacher.

ABOUT THE AUTHOR

BEN WOODWARD'S repeated personal experience with family trauma, chronic illness, and corporate crisis have taught and tutored him with intimate insight. The gained wisdom from such lessons have seen him thrive as a senior executive in multibillion-dollar companies, becoming the global president of a multinational corporation. He has served on the board of directors for trade associations, traveled to thirty countries as a keynote speaker, business leader, and entrepreneur, and most importantly, enjoys a wonderful home life with his wife Kim and seven beautiful children. To reach Ben, visit EmpowermentParadox.com.